ROGER FEDERER

First published in 2017
by Eyewear Publishing Ltd
Suite 38, 19-21 Crawford Street
London, W1H 1PJ
United Kingdom

Graphic design by Edwin Smet
Author photograph by Tim Jackson
Printed in England by TJ International Ltd, Padstow, Cornwall

*Eyewear wishes to thank Jonathan Wonham
for his generous patronage of our press.*

Set in Bembo 12 / 15 pt
ISBN 978-1-911335-24-5

WWW.EYEWEARPUBLISHING.COM

SQUINT
BOOKS

ROGER FEDERER

PORTRAIT
OF AN ARTIST

CHRISTOPHER JACKSON

 **EYEWEAR** PUBLISHING

For my mother,

*Lacrosse and netball champion, longstanding Wimbledon aficionado —
with apologies that this book constitutes the height of her son's sporting
achievements.*

AUTHOR'S NOTE

It has been my instinct to circle him. Though the text has a chronological element, it doesn't tell the strict story of Federer's life, match by match, year by year. Federer's life, in any case, is simply told. Like all his fellow players he committed to tennis very young. Over time he proved himself equal to the task of becoming a professional sportsman. Eventually he became the best in the world and then, on and off, the world's second-best. During that period he married, and became a father to two sets of twins. He amassed endorsements. He became exceedingly wealthy and started a foundation in his own name. All these things are referenced in the text. But I have also felt the need to zoom out, to approach him from other angles. In my first chapter I have sought to place his sport – his 'art' – in context. Even an apparently modern phenomenon like Federer is caught up in history, and needs to be understood in relation to it. The remaining chapters look at Federer in connection with beauty, morality, power, time, and meaning. They are riffs – circlings.

A word about the title. It is already a cliché that Federer is in some sense an artist. I am aware that it is dangerous to conflate two distinct terms – no one would seriously argue that, say, Michelangelo was a cricketer or that Wayne Rooney is painting a picture when he scores a goal. On the one hand, this book aims to unpick that confusion, and to discover how it has arisen. But it also takes the aesthetic pleasures that can be derived from sport seriously. The case of Federer becomes in these pages an investigation into wider questions. What role should sport play in our lives? What kind of attention should we give to it? So the book veers deliberately – into other sports, and areas of life, and into history – but the discussions always derive from Federer and always return to him. There is plenty of Federer here, but other things as well.

C.J., London, May 2017

Federer at Wimbledon in 2009 [1]

CHAPTER ONE – FEDERER AND HISTORY

Roger is just the greatest player of all time.
– John McEnroe

*Federer is the best player in history, no other player has
ever had such quality.* – Rafael Nadal

Looked at with certain eyes, is this not strange?

On a sunny day in 2012, twenty thousand people file into a huge room with a retractable roof in a leafy suburb of London. They are excitable, even raucous. In its environs, a glass of beer or champagne costs roughly double what you'd expect, and so do the strawberries, which for some reason are ubiquitous. Nobody minds these costs: some have already paid thousands of pounds to be here, and will not ruin their day by lamenting the additional expenditure. Television is here too – tens of millions of pairs of eyes are trained on what is about to unfold. But the cameras do not focus on the human interactions of the day, the friendships and the flirtations in the overpriced cafés and restaurants that surround the huge room. Instead interest centres on the room's contents: a green rectangle of grass, with white geometric lines painted on it. The nearer people get to this grassy patch, the giddier they become. Meanwhile, a large number of people go to a hill behind the big room to look at an image of this green rectangle on a hoisted screen, seemingly for the privilege of being physically nearby, though they cannot see the room's interior directly, and could easily get the same images at home.

At the appointed time, the crowd – inside and outside the big room – starts going berserk. Two tall confident-looking men, dressed in angelic white, walk out onto the green rectangle. One is Scottish, the other Swiss. Each carries a large pear-shaped bag. Normal in most respects – of average looks and normal intelligence – they nevertheless create pandemonium in their vicinity. Amid speculative murmur, the players produce rackets from their bags, and begin to hit a yellow ball over a net 0.914 metres in height. Throughout this, the crowd continues to chatter. The TV cameras concentrate on two suited men – in build, rather like the people on the rectangle of grass – being interviewed by a woman in a cream pantsuit. Then, apropos of nothing, a man in a high chair solemnly intones the word 'Time' into a microphone. At this, the crowd is whipped into hysteria. Some scream the name of the Scottish person. Others shout the name of the Swiss man as if they desperately needed something from him. A few moments ago, when they were hitting the ball over the 0.914-metre net, the process of hitting the ball could elicit no emotion from the crowd or the players. Now, everything that occurs causes outsized reactions in everyone assembled.

If a player hits a ball 78 feet, he reacts by punching the air. But if the same action goes 78 feet and a quarter of an inch, he will tear at his hair, or look as baffled as a man who has mislaid his credit card, or just missed his train.

As for the crowd, sometimes they wail with despair if the yellow ball hits the net. But if it hits the net and jumps over they all let out a large 'ooh'. If the ball travels at a sharp angle past a player's racket, the crowd emits a gigantic scandalised laugh. But if a very similar shot is hit more or less straight, the crowd will clap politely and nod as if at some expected pleasantry. As the afternoon progresses emotions increase: the crowd pleads more and more urgently with the players but never specifies its needs. Eventually, the Scottish man hits a shot over one of the white lines, and the Swiss man collapses in relief. The Scottish man walks towards the net with the demeanour of someone being led to his own execution. The Swiss man starts crying, and shakes the hand of the Scot and of the man who has been calling out the words 'Time' and 'Love', as well as the numbers 15, 30 and 40 throughout the afternoon, like some monotonous philosopher-cum-mathematician. The Swiss man seems happy and understandably so: after the match, he is given enough money not to have to work for a decade. The Scot, who is sad, is given about the same amount. Both then talk about what they have just done for the next five hours to people from most countries in the world. Then everyone goes home and begins the process of forgetting what they have seen.

The occasion, of course, is the Wimbledon final in 2012. The players are Andy Murray and Roger Federer.

How did all this come to be?

THE ORIGINS OF TENNIS

History is often silent about its pleasant inspirations: the sport Roger Federer plays has murky origins. We don't know who built the first racket or made the first court. There was no chronicler on hand to record the invention of the tramline or the net. No poet celebrated the tautening of the first strings.

Instead it rises out of a medieval mist, but we do at least have an inkling of where it comes from. In the modern game, the French Open is sometimes considered the least prestigious of tennis' four major tournaments. Many modern

greats have found it embarrassingly difficult to win at Roland
Garros (Federer) or have been forced to end superlative
careers without that title (John McEnroe, Boris Becker, Pete
Sampras). Nevertheless the historical record is insistent. The
game originates in northern France in the 1100s, as *jeu de
paume* – or game of the palm. Rackets didn't come in until
the sixteenth century. Even so, the red clay which has hosted
several unlikely champions from Gastón Gaudio to Thomas
Muster, and denied such a roll call of greats is, after a fashion,
home turf for the sport. Its origins provide another historical
parallel. Federer's great rival Rafael Nadal might be known
now as the King of Clay, but his sport's ancestor real tennis
was associated with actual kings. Louis XII, that adventurous
but inconsequential monarch, died of pneumonia after a
particularly vigorous game. James I of Scotland and Henry
VIII were also avid players. Federer's seven 'coronations' at
Wimbledon have their precursors in true kingship. In today's
tennis, commentators talk of players striving for glory, but it
has always been played by the glorious.

It might be a glitzy game, but it has paradoxically
been considered thoughtful – a game of guile as well as power.
When the game spread to England during the medieval period,
it first shows up on the record as played in monasteries. But
then even today the sport attracts the meditative and the
philosophically-minded. Roger Federer has been written
about by a slew of well-known writers from David Foster
Wallace and JM Coetzee to Julian Barnes and Clive James.
There might be more continuity about that than we know.
The ruined abbeys of this country, so cerebral-seeming, were
once perhaps prototypes of today's tennis clubs: outdoorsy
monks absconding from their prescribed round of meditation

and prayer to play tennis. Perhaps they had the sort of vigour that Chaucer gently mocked in the General Prologue to *The Canterbury Tales*. Chaucer's monk is a 'prikasour aright'[2] – that is to say, 'certainly a hunter' – who owns greyhounds, isn't desperately keen on a life of sequestration and longs for the physical life.

For centuries, people have looked on their day's tasks, found them not especially appetising, and opted instead for play.

UPON THE SERIOUSNESS (OR OTHERWISE) OF TENNIS

There has always been this conflict about sport. When we play or watch tennis, we are likely neglecting duties more important. This guilt accounts for the need many have to justify the attention they give to sport. Here is Simon Barnes, Federer aficionado and longstanding sportswriter for *The Times*, writing in the wake of the terror attacks in Paris in November 2015. He is responding to the fact that one of the bombs went off outside the Stade de France in Saint-Denis:

> People just won't take the advice of the commentators and accept that sport has no meaning. The idea that liking sport is a grave error of metaphysics doesn't seem to be holding up. Philosophers can produce a million arguments to show us that sport is appalling, futile, trivial, useless and worthless — but they can't stop the world loving the damn stuff.[3]

One isn't quite sure where these legions of philosophers are who would cancel all our leisure – although we shall meet some in these pages who would wish to question its value.

But the alleged unseriousness of tennis has a history stretching back some eight hundred years: we only know about those tennis courts in the Middle Ages because of the authorities' attempts to shut them down. Plainly, humankind is somewhat divided on the topic of play – how much of it should we have? It is odd that what gives pleasure should also cause angst.

Even so, if there has been a tendency to police leisure, there is a far richer history of people thumbing their noses at boring official injunctions. In the Renaissance and beyond, we begin to get hints of mass participation in Federer's sport. References to the game enter the Jacobean theatre with gratifying regularity: it is a lesson in the strange persistence of play. There is, for instance, John Webster's famous quote in *The Duchess of Malfi* (1612-3): 'we are merely the stars' tennis balls struck and bandied which way please them'[4]. In this line, tennis provides a metaphor for the possible futility of human life – but it also shows that the game was readily to hand as metaphor. The popularity of the sport could not escape the capacious curiosity of William Shakespeare: in *Henry V*, an ambassador from the Dauphin brings a case of tennis balls to mock King Henry who as a result quickly vows to attack France. Here tennis is still the sport of kings, but it leaps to the mind of the playwright son of a Stratford glover.

In spite of this, tennis remained a sport with a highly aristocratic image. Nowadays the Duke and Duchess of Cambridge are regularly to be found spectating at Wimbledon, peering down with discerning connoisseurship from the Royal Box. In those days it was the other way round: the kings and aristocrats were still taking to the court.

But interest had begun to trickle down.

THE YEAR OF THE LAWNMOWER

Tennis in our time has been to a large extent a tale of technical advances. Roger Federer's play, lauded for its beauty, would be less so, or beautiful in a different way, if it hadn't been for the 1980s' move away from wooden rackets to their graphite counterparts with larger heads and greater capacity for topspin.

But it might not have been at all, but for an important invention which can still be seen in London's Science Museum

Fig. 1. An advertisement for Ransomes' lawn-mower to a design by Edwin Budding. This invention was an im-portant milestone in the development of tennis.[5]

in Kensington. It is the world's first mechanical lawnmower, built by JR and A. Ransomes of Ipswich in 1832 to a design by a certain Edwin Budding (Fig. 1). Budding is one of those curious people in history who make the world a demonstrably happier place to little fanfare: his lawnmower was tailor-made for sporting grounds, and after it was introduced there was a marked expansion, financed by a growing middle class, of amateur sport. Budding may even deserve the title of minor visionary. Nobody else seems to have particularly felt that the lawns of England lay dormant and ready for golf, tennis, cricket and football. Budding did – and in realising this might even be said to have invented a new idea of England. The English summer, full of lazy activity and green leisure, is partly attributable to him. Wimbledon, scene of Federer's most vivid triumphs, would have been impossible without him.

1832 therefore feels like a useful cut-off point. If Budding guessed a widespread appetite for sport, he might not have foreseen the codification of the laws of many games which ensued as a result of his invention, and which over time would give us modern sport. The years following were a tale of drastic proliferation of amateur involvement; this trend morphed over time into the first professionals. No doubt if we could bring back the likes of Johann Wolfgang von Goethe and Walter Scott – both of whom died in 1832 – and place them in our era, they wouldn't recognise our world of lauded athletes, lucrative sponsorship deals, global television and round-the-clock coverage. Indeed, once they had come to terms with air travel and the Internet, the prevalence of sport might be one of their chief surprises. Would they approve or disapprove? Has our worship of sportsmen and women gone too far?

SPORT AND THE GREEKS

In looking closely at a figure like Roger Federer, we have the opportunity to connect with far remoter periods of history than Victorian England. This study would have seemed more usual to the ancient Greeks than to the early Victorians.

A simple – but essentially intellectual – pleasure in the exertions of the body was a part of Greek life. In Plato's (c.424-c.348 BC) book *The Laws* – his last dialogue in which a lifetime's reflection is crowded – his character The Athenian states that human beings should 'live out our days playing at certain games – sacrificing, singing, and dancing'[6]. For Aristotle (383-322 BC) in his *Politics* sport was a source of contemplation: for him, the image of the human being wholly immersed in play was, paradoxically, something to take very seriously indeed. Surveying ancient Greece, one finds little of our modern angst about whether we are wasting time when cheering on an Olympics or immersed in a tennis match. That is because they were looking at it differently. The Greeks were minded to praise the whole man – and that included physical activity as much as intellectual or spiritual endeavours. The Greek mind moved freely between associations. In the odes of Pindar (522-433BC) an Olympic victory can be used as a meditation on a range of things from myth and history, to family and poetry itself. Here, for instance, is the majestic beginning of Pindar's 'Olympian I':

> Water is pre-eminent and gold, like a fire
> Burning in the night, outshines
> All possessions that magnify men's pride.
> But if, my soul, you yearn
> To celebrate great games,

Look no further
For another star,
Shining through the deserted ether
Brighter than the sun, or for a contest
Mightier than Olympia...

[Pindar, Olympian I, 1-10][7]

In these few lines Pindar moves from the grandeur of a sporting occasion to reflections on the elements, human pride, and the stars. His is an orderly universe: the glory of being human is that we are permitted to roam in thought, and that whatever we are doing – even, though he wasn't aware of the game, when playing tennis – we are plugged in to a meaningful hierarchy. Nothing can ever be inconsequential: sport must partake of the overall cosmic drama because in this view of life the entire universe is charged, and resolutely alive. Is this something we have lost or are in danger of losing? In Saul Bellow's 1953 novel *The Adventures of Augie March*, the hero's predicament is that in an age of specialisation, he is not a specialist. Our world is more segregated even than Bellow's was: sport has its own tab on news websites, its own apportionment of our news bulletins. In our time, thoughts of Roger Federer lead all too often not to Pindar-like reflections on science, poetry and the stars, but to thoughts of Novak Djokovic.

In fact, if we have lost this capacity, then we lost it twice. Four centuries after his death, Pindar's poetry had been more or less lost. We are lucky to have any of it. Somewhere during the early Christian era there appears to have been a great swerve away from sport. This is not so surprising: there was a certain strain in Christianity – as there had been in Platonic philosophy – which denied the body. For all his physical vigour, it is difficult to imagine Saint Paul playing a game: the moral world was so urgent for him that only seriousness would do. The Desert Fathers, serious-minded and ascetic, do not come across as sporty. The neo-Platonic philosopher Plotinus (204-270) remarked that he was ashamed to have a body. The ensuing Dark Ages, with their numerous struggles and deprivations, provided less leisure.

As we have touched on, the Renaissance marked a return to play. Interestingly, this coincided with a renewed appreciation of the beauty of the human physique. This shall be looked at in more detail in Chapter Two. But by the twentieth century, an austere modernism had arisen in the arts: stern distinctions had been arrived at between high and low art. If a popular novel could be considered trashy, then that went also for sports. A certain snootiness about sport emerged. True, there were anomalies. Samuel Beckett, perhaps the most inscrutable of the moderns, is the only Nobel Laureate to have played first-class cricket*. Even so there are still people today who would claim that sport is largely meaningless: Christopher Hitchens would proudly state that it was the only area of life he had never published a piece about.

And yet the objections of a few didn't do anything to alter the behaviour of the many: whatever philosophers possess in gravitas, they tend to lose in audience.

---

* Beckett played twice for Dublin University in first-class fixtures, against Northamptonshire in 1925 and 1926. His love of the sport was continued by a host of dramatists including Harold Pinter, who started his own cricket team, and Tom Stoppard, who played wicket-keeper for the Pinter XI.

By 1877 Wimbledon had an annual tournament as well as its first champion in the shape of Spencer Gore. By the interwar period, players had become celebrities, and modern celebrity is the democratisation of fame. Sporting heroes emerged. In golf there was Harry Vardon. In cricket, there was WG Grace. And in the mid-1930s, tennis found its own anti-establishment hero when the un-aristocratic Fred Perry created a storm by winning Wimbledon. After his first Wimbledon triumph in 1934, he overheard a member of the club snobbishly complain, 'The best man didn't win'. What that member meant was that the best tennis player had turned out to be someone he hadn't met at a cocktail party. Perry's victory can be seen as another important moment in the long process of trickle-down in participation from kings to masses. Perry, in his affairs with the famous (he dated Marlene Dietrich) and in his decision to turn professional in 1936, was a harbinger of the modern era.

Roger Federer is typically difficult to pin down on this spectrum. He was born into the Swiss middle class, and as such is an emblem of the game's twentieth century expansion. But it has often been noticed that he plays the game with a certain hauteur, and a sort of stylish propriety which calls to mind the pre-Perry era.

THE MODERN PERSPECTIVE

In our time, the tension between those who find pleasure in sport and those who don't has been further compounded by the rise of the ardent sports fan: those who obsess about sports, or even a particular sport, to the exclusion of all else. Nick Hornby's *Fever Pitch* (1992) is a comic portrait of the obsessiveness of an Arsenal fan: it self-deprecatingly shows how all-encompassing the love of a single team can become. At the same time the proliferation of sport has made following it that much more time-consuming. In a sport much reported-about with a busy TV-driven calendar, keeping up with a team, or a player like Roger Federer, is a full-time job.

Why is there such demand and deep need? A few guesses will be hazarded. In a world which can appear chaotic and violent, sport provides welcome relief. In the teeming universe of the Internet, tennis is seen to vie with political crises, financial woes, health worries, and news of world business trends for our attention (Fig. 2). The feats of Roger

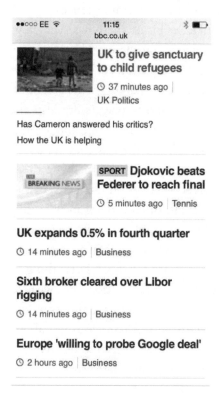

Fig. 2. Still from a mobile phone, January 2016. Tennis takes its place in our conscious-ness alongside political and economic worries.[8]

Federer come to us as our light relief from the misery of world affairs: they are bulletins from a less painful world. Its glitz suits the computerised image and, in turn, its prevalence is catching. Tennis' ties to money and corporate life render it an easy fit for newspapers and websites owned by billionaires. Furthermore, in the complex modern world, with the usual structures of religion, class and local life collapsing around us, many seek new modes of identification – in loving a football club, in the following of a sport, or in the cultivation of an obsession over a particular individual, we can become rooted in a world which seems always to be losing some portion of an original coherence: sport is reclamation of innocence.

Sport can also feel like *our* bit of the news. Very few of us will ever play the statesman alongside world leaders, but most of us know what it is to pick up a cricket bat or a tennis racket. Today's fans are enthusiastic amateurs who dream of partaking in what they observe. Sports players are also *our* celebrities. We have journeyed alongside them, and rooted for them, in a way which we haven't for our film stars and musicians, who sometimes seem, by their aloofness, up there on the screen, and by their freedom to enter character or the creative space, not to need us at all. But a Federer in an empty stadium – a Federer without us – would not really be Federer at all. We create the spectacle by which he thrives; we create the conditions of his experiment with the sport. Everything in our modern world, whether it be our fascination with wealth, our love of occasion, our hunger for celebrity, and even our need of quick pleasures and morbid self-consciousness about our health, has contrived to make sport central to our lives.

But though sport seems implicated in the superficiality of modern life, the sports arena is still a place where the miraculous can impinge. Our sportsmen and sportswomen are our modern heroes. They have taken outrageous gambles on our behalf, sacrificing the easy office-life for a stab at glory. They have toiled hugely, and have asserted that the ordinary isn't satisfactory for them. They provide us with moments of stunning achievement and memorable theatre. Our appetite is increased by the fleetingness of these moments: even the most superb Wimbledon final flickers before us and is gone, creating in the process our need for next year's final. The transience of a great sporting moment magnifies the sacrifice involved. The great rugby union fly-half Johnny Wilkinson trained on Christmas Day year after year for that winning drop goal in the 2003 Rugby World Cup Final, a gleam of splendour which nevertheless will recede eventually in the collective memory. Sport calls to mind the evanescence of all life. Much more likely a sportsperson will work at enormous cost and exertion toward a career which will eventually prove deficient in glory. Most Olympians and lower-ranked players across professional sport must be sustained largely by love of the task itself: if sport can ever be seriously compared to art, then it is usually an art for art's sake. Our inherent interest in personality completes the picture. While we watch, we note the types of human material ranged before us. We have the precocious but squandered talent (George Best, Tracy Austin), the tragic hero (Tiger Woods), the principled straight man (Jordan Spieth), the fearless warrior who makes his own rules (Zinedine Zidane), the comic hero (Usain Bolt).

And in tennis alone we have the gritty fighter (Murray), the superman (Djokovic), untiring brawn (Nadal), the temperamental genius (Safin), the gallant loser (Roddick), and the bad-boy villain (Kyrgios).

And we also have the dandified artist.

THE ACHIEVEMENT OF FEDERER

If sport is one of the main preoccupations of our modern world, then Roger Federer's long career, even in its unfinished state, must be one of the wonders of it.

As impressive as his achievements themselves is the style in which they have come about. The 1980s had seen a high point for the sport. The magnificently temperamental American John McEnroe had enjoyed a rivalry of contrasts with the profoundly calm Swede Björn Borg, producing the memorable 1980 Wimbledon final. This had ceded, via Borg's early retirement, and the impressive careers of Boris Becker and Stefan Edberg, to the dichotomous era of big-serving Pete Sampras and baseliner Andre Agassi: both players, great in their respective ways, were nearing the twilight of their careers by the time Roger Federer came along. Agassi had played a game of groundstrokes full of steady wizardry, but Sampras – the slightly more successful of the two – had dominated with a powerful serve which was very difficult to break. Seeing his success, many of Sampras' rivals did the same. The game seemed to bifurcate along these two themes – in the direction of the server on the one hand with his grim aces and eked-out tie breaks, and the baseliner on the other, usually of inferior height but with greater sleight of hand, who could return the unreturnable, and then manage to hold a less potent serve. Usually the server was the victor, because as a game plan it was less risky: with a less powerful serve, the diminutive Agassi looked at an unfair disadvantage. His victories, when they came, were appealing because they appeared to go against the grain of modern competition. With their stylishness, and their seeming advocacy of variety, they were a foretaste of Federer's wins. Tennis had become a power sport, especially suitable for the tall athlete.

Roger Federer entered this era of big serving. Matches could sometimes pass in a saga of endless aces and mishit returns. The nadir of this was probably Michael Stich's ace-riddled Wimbledon win in 1991. If Federer is an artist then he is one of those rare ones who will leave his art unrecognisable from how he found it – he has, as John Arlott said of Jack Hobbs, 'reshaped the history of bat and ball'[9]. In place of monotonous serving backed by intimidating excursions to the net, Federer plays a tennis which marries the variety of the wooden rackets era of the 1960s with the dizzying pace of the modern game. The forehand is whipped and ingenious, and attractive to watch. But there is nothing sedate about it: it is instead a thing of sound and fury. The serve is absurdly effective but never monotonous. His backhand slice is scuddingly cunning. He is a superb 'touch' volleyer. Armed with these strokes, as well as a Fred Astaire nimbleness about the court and a mountaineer's calm in difficult situations, Federer appeared for a while to have the perfect game. It was, above all – to quote Arlott on Hobbs again – 'a balanced art'[10].

Like this, Federer enters history – sponsored by the medieval inventors of the game, and with the air of a modern king, and looking very much like the sort of Greek athlete Pindar might have been inclined to praise. It is appealing to imagine that he represents some sort of synthesis or culmination for his sport.

Alongside these precursors and associations, his actual achievements can read somewhat statistically. But there is no harm in reciting them. Roger Federer has 18 Grand Slam titles (more than any other male player) and has spent a record 302 weeks as the world's number one player (also a record). He has won all four major championships, a feat not achieved by John McEnroe, Pete Sampras or Björn Borg. From 2003 until his defeat in the 2008 final to Rafael Nadal, Federer was undefeated at Wimbledon, and now has more Wimbledons (seven) than any other modern player. He appeared in 18 out of 19 finals from the 2005 Wimbledon final through to the 2010 Australian Open.

Federer's statistics are impressive, of course, and many others might be cited. But they have a way of blurring into one another. It might be better simply to say that Federer has won more than anyone has ever won and has also done it in greater style. He has also been doing it now for an extraordinarily long time. By the 2016 Australian Open he had appeared in a record 47 Grand Slam tournaments, a tribute to a high level of play sustained over many years; his astonishing win at the 2017 Australian Open saw Federer become the second oldest winner of a Grand Slam title. He has continued long past the point when his original contemporaries, Hewitt and Roddick, Safin and Nalbandian, have retired. In fact, until that 2017 win in Melbourne, one wondered whether he was persisting beyond the point where it was likely he would add significantly to his place in the game. Instead he displays that commitment to a task, that love of something for its own sake, which has often earned him the epithet of 'artist'. After the 2017 Australian Open final, Federer was relaxed about its statistical importance: 'For me it's all about the comeback, about an epic match with Rafa again. The last problem is the Slam count. Honestly, it doesn't matter.'[11] Style in sport often comes at a certain cost: there are few more beautiful golf swings than Fred Couples', for instance, and yet it is the workmanlike, gym-going Tiger Woods who really takes the laurels*. Federer's greatness has come with few concessions: he never wins unattractively. It is true that Nadal and Djokovic both have a winning record over him. Djokovic may well finish with more Grand Slams and more weeks at number one on the ATP Tour. But neither has been so adored, because neither has yet been able to place such vivid images of pure excellence in our minds. His opponents have frequently remarked on the ludicrous facility with which he plays the game. It may be that he doesn't mind as much as we do about his cultural significance; he can sometimes seem baffled as to why he gives such pleasure to people. The strange fact cannot be avoided: by becoming exceptionally good at a simple game, he has become a figure with a certain historical importance.

And to begin to understand Federer's place in the world, it is necessary to look closer at this idea of beauty.

---

* Not in any way to denigrate Couples, a marvellous golfer, and the winner of the 1992 US Masters.

CHAPTER TWO – FEDERER AND BEAUTY

That Roger Federer plays exceptionally attractive tennis
is a truth that is widely – if not universally acknowledged.
But opinions differ as to what to make of this fact.
– William Skidelsky, *Federer and Me: A Story of Obsession*

'Tis not a lip, or eye, we beauty call,
But the joint force and full result of all.
– Alexander Pope, *Essay on Criticism*

In René Stauffer's book *The Roger Federer Story: Quest for Perfection*, the author provides us with a brief close-up of life around Federer when he was growing up. Today he might move smoothly from tennis to media appearances in numerous languages, before switching to philanthropy or family life, but what emerges here, in the dark backward and abysm of time, is a tale of monomania. It might read tragically were it not the precursor to such absurd success.

> For hours, Roger hit tennis balls against a wall, a garage door, in his room against a wall or even against the cupboard in the house. Pictures and dishes were not safe and his sister's room wasn't spared either.[12]

The repetition of the phrase 'against the wall' provides, perhaps by a proofreader's negligence, the right impression. Everything begins in this domestic scene in the home of a Swiss lab technician. The vital components are already there:

ball and trajectory, racket and direction. And there is also the player himself trying to master these. Other variables will be added later on. There will be the different surfaces: the looping bounce of clay which will give him such difficulty against Rafael Nadal, and the low-bouncing idiosyncrasies of grass which will be used to great advantage at Wimbledon. There will be wind, like the violent one which he will master against Andre Agassi in the 2005 US Open final; or the darkness which will just fail to save him in the 2008 Wimbledon championship match. Crowds will come to see him: over the years they will be on his side throughout the world, but they will bring with them incalculable pressure, which he will usually master. Most importantly of all, time will bring him hundreds of opponents – those he will be in awe of like Sampras, those he can dominate like Roddick or Hewitt, those he must be patient with like big-serving Ivo Karlović, and vexatious opponents like Nadal and, later on, Djokovic.

But for now, it is just this. It will turn him into someone else – into an athlete, and then a rich and famous man, a fashion icon, and a philanthropist.

Great success at one thing can make it easy for someone to seem like a man of many talents later on. In this passage, we get a glimpse of what life has really been for Federer. To a degree that might surprise us, it has been about hitting tennis balls. There is something trusting and innocent about it. He will become rich enough to start his own foundation. Anna Wintour will design clothes for him. His opinion will be sought on world affairs. The narrowness of the task conceals improbable horizons. All great achievement begins with a quiet act of faith: *This is worth doing – this is what I'm good at.*

We do not have beauty yet but we have its possibility.

THE EARLY FOOTAGE

Is his gift inherited or acquired? It is both. Early footage of the young Federer[13] shows the same confident skip into the forehand and he goes at the ball with the same inimitable swish as he will later do. But it also shows how far he has to go: he has still to grow into his body, his spindly legs cannot quite raise him to the bounce of the ball; he doesn't hit through the ball as ferociously as we know he will. What is rudimentary is not beautiful. Young Federer also – famously – lacked serenity. There is old footage of Federer's lost temper as a boy: he gestures with despair at a ball gone awry, or protests the broken promise of a missed forehand. Nowadays, he is silent when he misses, and rarely does more than cancel the memory of the error and recuperate. In these early frames, Federer exhibits what he has subsequently managed to conceal: a fierce will to do well at this. Federer now channels his emotion into a slow combing of hair round the right ear, as if he wants to verify it is still the same shape as it was before the missed shot. What motivates him in this early footage is not the hope of career and future money and endorsements, or even perhaps a short-term competitive need. It is something purer: a love of the thing itself. In every missed forehand or thrown racket, you can see it plain: he wants intention and execution to link up satisfactorily. Purity is one of the leitmotifs of Federer's career. In later years he will express disdain for the Hawk-eye system of line calls, since it creates jerks and pauses in an entertainment which ought to run smoothly: here this fastidiousness is seen in its beginnings.

Of course, there are obvious limits to this purity. Already in this early footage, the will to win is there. But with Federer, one sometimes suspects that he wants to win primarily so as to play more tennis. In the early rounds of tournaments, at the moment of victory, one often feels he is simply relieved to be able to be back on court in a few days' time: he has won another commission. It is true that his career will be full of the jubilation of victory and occasionally involve him reaching for the philosophy of defeat. But throughout the natural ups and downs of a player's career, one has a sense that for Federer a simple love of the task at hand has, to an unusual degree, always persisted. Federer in his seamlessness reminds one of Zinedine Zidane, who is a good example of a sportsman who has thought deeply about what it is to play a sport to a high level and can indeed sound like a rapt artist: 'Sometimes I don't know what takes me over during a game. Sometimes I just feel I have moved to a different place and I can make the pass, score the goal or go past my marker at will.'* Federer's own descriptions of his tennis can be comparatively disappointing. In post-match interviews, Federer rarely strays beyond the bounds of polite platitude. His stated goal is to win, and the bigger the match the sweeter victory will seem to him. But there is an obvious delight in the game he plays, which is separate from mere outcome. Often when he loses he will say something to the effect that he had 'a good time tonight' or that it was 'a fun match'. This attitude inoculates him a little against defeat.

Federer's tennis reminds us that there is nothing wrong at all with incidental beauty. Most beauty – in nature, or in people – has an element of accident and surprise. Saul Bellow wrote in *Herzog*: 'Beauty is not a human invention'[14] – instead it often comes our way unasked-for, as a thing bestowed. The

---

* The film *Zidane: A 21ˢᵗ Century Portrait* (2006) concentrates only on Zidane's movements and decisions throughout one entire 90-minute game.

beauty of Federer's play arises in the context of competition, but like his own love of the game, it is independent of context: it is pure motion, pure form. There is a corollary to this: art has always been inherently competitive. The history of the Italian Renaissance can be told as a series of *paragone* – head-to-head match-ups between artists. Michelangelo, Leonardo and Raphael were quite as capable of being competitive with one another as Federer, Nadal and Djokovic. Ancient Greek playwrights rose to prominence on the back of winning competitions. We wouldn't have heard of Aeschylus, Sophocles or Euripides if they had been without the competitive instinct. One way to watch Federer, then, is to divorce yourself from minding about the result, and to watch it as a thing done for its own sake, as one might a dance.

As a boy, while he wasn't playing, young Federer became a connoisseur, and he is still known as a 'student' or alternatively 'historian' of the game. Boris Becker's Wimbledon win in 1985 captivated him; and his future coach Edberg and eventual friend Sampras became his heroes. Today, when Federer faces the younger players, he can look professorial, as if he is critiquing their tennis. Again, there is this fastidiousness about Federer, as if he were saying, 'This thing, tennis, regardless of whether I win or lose, should be done this way and not any other'.

'BOISTEROUS MEN'

One feature of the early footage is its ghostly quality, its spacious silence – as if those practice sessions were somehow, in a corner of the universe, still going on.

But silence is, of course, not something one associates

with sport. The stillness of that early footage – the startling lack of crowds and applause – would turn in time, via years of effort, to the din of the stadium. But it is this success, and the noise that comes with it, which can sometimes make it an uneasy fit with notions of beauty. We associate beauty with the musty corridors of the museum: the quiet shuffle of feet, the murmured nods of approval. It was this, for instance, which appears to have particularly irritated George Orwell about sport, when he wrote in his famous article 'The Sporting Spirit':

> The significant thing is not the behaviour of the players but the attitude of the spectators: and, behind the spectators, of the nations who work themselves into furies over these absurd contests, and seriously believe – at any rate for short periods – that running, jumping and kicking a ball are tests of national virtue.[15]

Orwell's disciple the late Christopher Hitchens seconded this, writing in an article for *The Guardian* that: 'Sport is guaranteed to stir up foul play'[16]. We shall look at this issue of morality in detail in the next chapter, but for now it is enough to say that the way sport comes to us can give us an excuse not to bestow our full attention: the beauty of Federer's play takes place not within the hallowed corridors of the gallery, but within the braying arena. But Pindar, interestingly, has a beautiful riposte to the Orwell-Hitchens critique of sport in his second Olympian ode:

> But praise falls short of surfeit
> And is muted, not in justice
> But because of boisterous men, whose noise

Would obscure beauty,
                    For sands cannot be counted
And how many joys
This man has brought his fellows,

                    Who can say?

                              [Olympian II, 93-100]

Perhaps Pindar's 'boisterous men' need not only be the typical
hooligans of our time, boringly enraged by the loss of a
football match, but also those who noisily ask us to think of
sport as meaningless, as a mere waste of time. Pindar's words
might instead nudge us towards another way of looking at
sport: it can be watched for its beauty and emotional power –
'the joys' it can bring us.

In fact some already watch sport – and in particular
Federer – in this way. Here, for instance, is the great South
African novelist JM Coetzee in correspondence with the
American novelist Paul Auster:

> One starts by envying Federer, one moves from there to
> admiring him and one ends up neither envying him or
> admiring him but exalted at the revelation of what a human
> being – a being like oneself – can do.[17]

If one were to substitute the name Federer for the names
Leonardo da Vinci or Johann Sebastian Bach the sentence
would still make perfect sense.

This, then, is what young Federer became: both a
sportsman and a purveyor of beauty. Conventional schooling

was refused. Football was decided against; tennis was doubled down upon. The talent did not – as in hundreds of other cases – find any particular ceiling. Instead it insisted on itself through the quiet glory of the boys' circuit, culminating in his junior Wimbledon title in 1998. Federer turned pro, to no fanfare, that year. By 1999, he had entered the Top 100. By 2000, Federer had reached (and lost) his first final. He proceeded to win the 2002 Hamburg Masters against Marat Safin, clinching his first title.

There were still irritating losses to be dealt with around that time, most notably his first round loss at Wimbledon in 2002 to Mario Ančić. There remains a sense among die-hard fans that perhaps he should have won more, sooner. But financial security was more or less reached even by this early stage in his career. And again, the statistics and the narrative can seem poor when set against another fact. All the while he was making these strides, Federer was also doing something more important: he was becoming immune to ugliness.

But if beautiful, then in what sense?

THE FEDERER SERVE AND FOREHAND

It's one of the most famous sights in modern sport: the so-called Federer one-two. It's worth looking at in detail.

First, the serve (Fig. 3). Roger Federer's ball toss is famously reliable and, opponents attest, frustratingly difficult to read. This most important shot in tennis requires both racket skill through the serving arm, and a steady left hand at the throw. Many of the most important moments in matches hinge on the ability to throw the ball calmly, to retain synchrony of movement under pressure. Like many of

Fig. 3. The Federer serve.[19]

his fellow pros, Federer has never grown tired of this simple task: he places the serving ball neatly on the V of the racket head, and then his body coils into springiness, settling into a mechanical pleasure. At the release of the ball, the fingers splay slightly as if offering up some gift, pointing skywards near the moment of contact. As the right arm comes down and over, the mind is full of guile, deciding what deception to practise on his opponent – what kind of spin to place on the ball, and what depth to aspire to. If delivering the serve from the deuce court, the ball might fly arrow-straight towards the T, leaving his opponent with a desperate dive to his left – the dive as ungainly as the serve was smooth. The 'out wide' serve will cause his opponent to lunge rightwards, the hand and racket outstretched, like a juggler who has gone out of position.

As soon as Federer serves he becomes a dancer, either

scuttling back behind the baseline or coming forwards, scanning the court for the result of his serve. Federer's adversary will sometimes manage to loop the ball back unconvincingly into the midcourt. In those situations, Federer will skip forwards, assessing the whereabouts of the ball with calm imperiousness, before readying himself with another flicker of feet for its arrival. He will then dispatch it either into an open court or back behind his opponent, wrong-footing him. It all takes about three seconds. It is always done while remaining silent: the performance has the look of a Greek statue permitted motion.

In an art of endless repetition and minor variation, the viewer's attention becomes minuter: Federer fans – and sports fans generally – become acclimatised to small details. Watching sport can become a way – to use John Updike's phrase – of 'giving the mundane its beautiful due'[18]. There is a known aesthetic pleasure in this. In looking at a series of Degas' ballet dancers, for instance, the viewer responds to minor adjustments in lighting or in the number or arrangements of figures to come into a deeper sense of what it means to be a ballet dancer, or to observe a ballet dancer, than one isolated picture could give you. The same is true of George Stubbs and his horses, where small changes in the frieze of animals orchestrate the viewer's emotional response. Likewise the viewer of a Federer tennis match responds to small distinctions. On a summer's day at Wimbledon, the sight of Federer can have a celestial feel: white clothes moving along lush grass. The black Federer tends to wear in New York can give the action a pantherish quality (Fig. 4). On clay – at the French Open or at Monte Carlo – the ball travels along a Martian terrain to pock the surface (Fig. 5). Sometimes an ace will hit the backboards with a pleasing thud, or a lines judge will expressionlessly tilt their head to avoid the ball. The dynamics of the movement are also altered by the opponent: in the early rounds, directed against inferior players, his serve has a mercilessness about it. Against the top players it reaches a higher peak of intensity and urgent movement. The moment in the match also has its bearings on what we see. If the serve in question happens to be a match point in his favour, he will smile bashfully once the point is over: except in cases of a stressful victory, he will be wryly sheepish at the misery he has inflicted on the other player. He will even seem sad that the match is over, to have lost his connection with that particular day. If at match point down, the slick operation is defiant, refusing all the contrary pressure ranged against it, like a Ferrari driving into a storm. On a championship point, it is at the height of its power, but also soon to be retired until the next tournament.

THE FRAGILITY OF BEAUTY

Federer's service action is endlessly interesting perhaps because it is inherently fragile. In an article for *The New Yorker* entitled 'Anxiety on the Grass', Calvin Tomkins wrote: 'Some people are so enthralled by the way Roger Federer plays tennis that they can hardly bear to see him lose'[22]. These emotions might be caused by a certain delicacy Federer has, a mixture of ballet and deception, which can be seen in microcosm in the serve-forehand combination. When we watch Federer lose to the superior muscle of Rafael Nadal, for example, we are faced with an image of beauty dismantled, like a butterfly pinned to a wall. One can recall the famous lines from Shakespeare's Sonnet 65:

Figs. 4 and 5. Variations upon a theme. The 'pantherish' black (above)[20] and the 'Martian terrain'[21] of the French Open (below).

> How with this rage shall beauty hold a plea
> Whose action is no stronger than a flower?[23]

Beauty is vulnerable because it is rare. We are witnessing something that cannot last forever. As we shall see in Chapter Five, even Federer's career has a clock on it. But perhaps there are other reasons for the strong attraction of Federer's tennis. As our busy and raucous lives unfold in our frenetic cities, perhaps Federer's brand of beauty is especially unusual. Put simply, there is a lack of beauty in our culture. Modern art, whether it be Emin's *My Bed* (Fig. 15) or Hirst's medicine cabinets, can sometimes seem to take a perverse pleasure in being intentionally squalid and ugly. Our films – our horrors and thrillers, romcoms and noirs – are not often beautiful. They are dins, extended ironies, bloodbaths, scares. To watch the Federer one-two is to experience the spectacle of a human body celebrating itself, clicking into a task, facing down pressure – arranging itself into a sight of flowing movement and capable form.

Federer is in direct juxtaposition to prevailing trends, first in producing beauty where we might not particularly expect to find it – in the slug and slog, and creaturely intensity, of a tennis match. But he is also an example of beauty in an age that lacks it.

But we haven't always lacked it, and it is this which might account for the obsessive way in which many watch Federer. It might be that his tennis engenders a form of nostalgia; it answers to ancient yearnings. There is a longstanding desire to look on the athletic human body in perfect synchrony: to watch a great athlete at work is to feel that however many discrepancies and faults there might be in our own bodies, we at least belong to a species which has the capacity to operate smoothly. To be physical is not necessarily – or not only – to be consigned to a lifetime of deprivation, awkwardness and decay. It is also a gigantic opportunity to dance, and run, and twist, and lurch, to shed tedium and to explore the potential of one's being in the open light.

THE GREEK IDEAL

The history of art is in fact – if we so wish – the story of human beings coming into this realisation. To look at the way in which the body has been represented throughout time will be to travel a little from Roger Federer but it will give some indication of the sort of pleasure people take in watching him play.

In Egyptian civilisation, we sometimes witness a certain desire for delicacy, in the fine features of a pharaoh, or in the exquisite animals on a tomb's exterior, but we do not yet see movement: there is, for instance, the typical depiction of Ramesses II with his curved cheekbones and cat-like look. Ramesses is refined; we can conceive of him as a person of impeccable taste. But Egyptian sculptures are, of course, monumentally static. The pharaoh is depicted as a god – seated, inscrutable (Fig. 6). Sculptures like this are intended to inspire awe, which is to say they intentionally reject sympathy: the viewer is meant to feel inferior. The Egyptians would not have known it at the time but in light of what came later, the modern viewer might feel that something is lacking.

It was the Greeks who first depicted the relationship between parts. It might be said that in doing so, they were depicting the democratic ideal: the human being takes the

Fig. 6. Ramesses II. Still and inscrutable – mobile beauty was unknown in Egyptian art.[24]

place of the pharaoh-god. It is a sort of sculptural precursor of the modern sporting ideal: anybody can enter. In early Greek statues, as in the *Kritios Boy* (Fig. 7), musculature becomes plausible. It is as if people suddenly understood that everything interconnects: the torso is nothing without the arms and legs. To be realistic about the condition of the body was to articulate the fact of interior flow: muscles must correspond, parts cohere, and everything measure up. But early statues like the *Kritios Boy*, although more truthful in their conception of how the body maps together than anything the Egyptians had been able to do, do not depict activity. It is hard to imagine the *Kritios Boy* coming to life. The energy is all to do with internal relationships – the working potential of the body is shown, but movement isn't yet a possibility. In retrospect we can see that looking on the naked body of a still athlete turned out to be an incomplete pleasure.

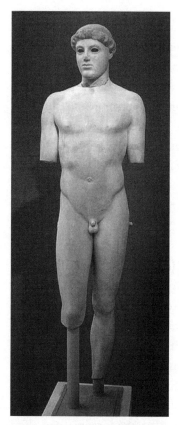 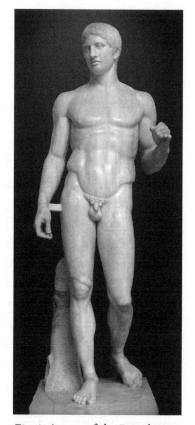

Fig. 7. *Kritios Boy*. Marble, c. 480 BC, Acropolis Museum, Athens. The viewer can take pleasure in the harmonious arrangement of the body but this figure doesn't move.[25]

Fig. 8. A copy of the *Doryphoros* in the Naples National Archaeological Museum. The original by Polykleitos was revolutionary: now, we have movement.[26]

This falling short seems obvious to us now, but we can be sure it wasn't then. Somewhere around 480 BC the wonderful occurred: a genius came along and the human body in sculpture began to move. This was Polykleitos (fifth century BCE), and we know frustratingly little about him. But in his sculptures – as in the *Doryphoros*, a copy of which can now be seen in the Naples National Archaeological Museum (Fig. 8) – the athlete is now caught in a position between repose and walking forwards. It was one of those quiet revolutions which alter the course of an art: motion has become something to concentrate on, and to marvel at. There was more to come. The sculptor Myron (active between 480 BC and 440 BC), in his famous *Diskobolos* (or The Discus Thrower) (Fig. 9) showed a naked athlete throwing a discus, the body stooped and set to uncoil, and the concentrating face wholly committed to his task.

Like all great advances, it seems obvious in retrospect: perhaps the signature characteristic of the human body is that it moves – it *works*. The specificity of the task is interesting: the viewer is no longer invited to look on the basic fact of stepping forwards, as in the *Doryphoros*, but on a complicated but arbitrary sporting motion: it might as well be a tennis serve. These Greek sculptures in their cheerful celebration of creation are easy to take for granted now: great art always appropriates a retrospective look of inevitability. But they may have fulfilled a different need for the Greeks than they do in today's viewer. Here is the art historian Kenneth Clark:

> We all have a mental picture of that strange institution, Greek athletics…Greek athletes competed in somewhat the same poetical and chivalrous spirit as knights, before the eyes of their loves, jousted in the lists: but all that pride and devotion which medieval contestants expressed through the flashing symbolism of heraldry, concentrated in one object, the naked body.[27]

For us, the bodies of Greek art strain or twist against the forces of the world. They might make us reflect on the nature of the human body, or inspire general thoughts about our place in the world. But to understand what Greeks felt before them one must imagine watching Roger Federer not just as an emblem of athletic excitement but also as a cause of love and a reason for religious faith. This will be difficult if one is not in love with Roger Federer or if one is disinclined to see his tennis as a proof of the existence of God. However, it is worth bearing in mind that beauty for the Greeks was never a purely isolated thing: it stood in relation to other things – faith, friendship and love. We shall further explore the meaning of sport in Chapter Six. Even so, standing before a Myron or a Polykleitos, the Greeks must have felt something like what Coetzee described to Auster in relation to Federer – 'revelation of what a human being – a being like oneself – can do'. And the *Diskobolos* does in fact look remarkably similar to stills one sees of the Federer forehand (Fig. 10): each has a still

Fig. 9. Copy of Myron's *Diskobolos*, 460-450 BC, British Museum.[28]

Fig. 10. A typical still of the Federer forehand, similar in many respects to the *Diskobolos*.[29]

head, and is wholly and mysteriously engaged in his pursuit. They are not the same thing of course – it hardly needs stating that the modern tennis player is clothed, for instance – but they might be said to answer to similar emotions.

We saw in the first chapter how an interest in sport went away during the Christian era and the Dark Ages only to resurface during the late medieval period and the Renaissance. This is exactly tracked in the history of art. Just as Pindar went out of fashion so, in time, did Greek sculpture.

After the fall of the Roman Empire, much was forgotten. Byzantine art would show idealised Christs, with dark-eyed gazes intended to produce awe and submission. Gothic art is reminiscent of early Egyptian art in its stiltedness, and in its creation of anatomically impossible forms: one is left with an impression of a certain loss of delight at the sheer physicality of things.

THE RENAISSANCE

But the power of the Greek nude was only in temporary retreat: when the Renaissance came it was really this that was being rediscovered. That rediscovery can be traced today in the Uffizi Gallery in Florence: as you walk through the centuries, the Christs and Virgin Marys begin to move again; motion is possible once more. In a famous *Annunciation* (Fig. 11) by Simone Martini (1284-1344), the Madonna swerves away from the arriving Gabriel. After years of static doe-eyed Christs, it is rather a relief: the world has reawakened to a consciousness of its own fluidity. But even so, this movement is different to the Greek kind: over a thousand years of Christianity could not be wiped away so easily. In Renaissance art, movement is always allied to Christian drama. In Renaissance Depositions, for instance, when a dead Christ is shown slumping towards the ground, we are seeing both the realistic movement that occurs when gravity acts on a dead body taken down from a cross, but also the pity of the situation. In later religious

Fig. 11. Martini, *Annunciation* (1333). Uffizi, Florence. Things begin to move again.[30]

art – most noticeably in Raphael (1483-1520) and Leonardo da Vinci (1452-1519) – physical movement is still secondary. What matters is what is happening on the spiritual plane, and at the level of grace. The art is essentially dualistic. The inward landscape is as important as what is seen: what is striven *for* is more important than how striving *looks*. Vigorous physical activity might be seen to be truculence or a turning away from the spiritual life. Physical depletion might be spiritually warranted and even revelatory. There is not quite the same bursting sense of unmitigated physical health that you get in the Greek ideal. Of course, this is one way in which Renaissance art, particularly for a Christian, can seem superior to its Greek counterpart: it is only to say that it doesn't cater entirely to the particular Grecian appetite, and that for some this might be taken for a lack.

Fig. 12. Botticelli's *La Primavera* (c. 1482), Uffizi Gallery, Florence: the return of beauty and movement for its own sake.[31]

Throughout the first part of the Quattrocento, painters (and, as importantly, patrons) never forgot that there had to be a religious dimension to art. But a craze for the ancients was in the offing and gradually, as the reign of Lorenzo the Magnificent (1449-1492) with his love of all things Greek took hold, a neo-paganism for a brief marvellous moment became the fashion. The human body at movement was enjoyed again for its own sake, and celebrated on account of its raw potential. Sandro Botticelli (c. 1445-1510) in works like *La Primavera* produced female figures who form part of allegories so cryptic that one ends up looking at his bodies with a pleasure independent of the context of the painting (Fig. 12). Of course, there is still a Platonic dimension, but with the Christian story absented, there is an unmistakeable rushing in of light and room. We are outdoors again, and in the wide open – and where dance is in the offing, athletics is never far behind. Other developments ensued. It was Michelangelo (1475-1564) who more than any other artist proved equal to the Greek ideal and even took it further: his gigantic *David* (Fig. 13) stood for centuries outside the Palazzo Vecchio as an assurance to the world that human beings are capable of godlike enormity: as a rendition of heroism it might be said to be quasi-Egyptian, but his knowledge of figure and musculature was Grecian. This finds its parallel in modern sport. Anyone who attends a major tennis tournament notes how tall and impressive the likes of Djokovic and Federer are in real life: they too, facing down immense pressure and projecting considerable fame, are emblems of the heroic and what is possible for human beings. We shall return to *David* again in the next chapter.

To complete the picture, the *Mercury* by Giambologna (1529-1608) (Fig. 14) is as finely balanced as a gymnast, his hand pointing heavenwards while he stands on tiptoe. We are faced in this miraculous piece with a calm but ecstatic collusion between body and mind, not unlike a tennis player reaching upwards at a critical moment to make an important overhead smash.

Fig. 13. Michelangelo's *David* (1501-4), Galleria dell'Accademia. An image of the hero.[32]

Fig. 14. Giambologna, *Mercury* (1564-5), Bargello Museum. From this angle, reminiscent of an overhead tennis smash.[33]

THE DECLINE OF BEAUTY AND MOTION IN ART

From such pinnacles there can only be decline. As the High Renaissance shaded into the Baroque, the plastic arts became divorced from focussed movement: grandiosity and pattern for its own sake became the dominant modes.

Over time, artists began to experiment with a neo-Gothic elongation of form. For instance in the works of the painter known as El Greco (1541-1614), the bodies already have pointed chins and a sort of funny-mirror misshapenness: they might belong on the West Front of Chartres Cathedral. The pleasure of the body was often ignored in favour of exploring its drawbacks and ills. In Rembrandt (1606-1669) for instance, the presiding interest is in the minutiae of the ageing process.

In place of fresh confidence came gritty determination. In the work of Ingres (1780-1867), anatomical errors begin to creep in: his *Odalisque* in the Louvre, for instance, lazily lovely though she is, has an impossibly long spine. In the paintings of Eugène Delacroix (1798-1863), the figure began to blur: human beings in his pictures appear as pessimistic swirls of atoms which must soon pass away. In important respects, Delacroix was influential. As the nineteenth century drew on, the figure blurred further, and Impressionism was born. In the works of Pierre-Auguste Renoir (1841-1919) and Edgar Degas (1834-1917) figures are still ephemeral. Renoir (Fig. 15) very rarely shows the body in motion; Degas' ballet dancers, however wonderfully they might twirl and swirl, look like they are about to melt into thin air. For both artists, reality is insubstantial. Rembrandt, Delacroix and the Impressionists all produced beautiful pictures, but one dreams before them – they do not make one celebrate the body as the Greeks did

Fig. 15. Pierre-Auguste Renoir, *La Liseuse* (1875), Musée d'Orsay. An example of the Impressionist move away from Greek form and movement towards blur and stillness.[34]

before a Myron, or as Coetzee does when watching Roger Federer.

Impressionism was predominantly a still art; it is full of lazy sun, and slow days in Provence. In looking so closely at the world – whether in the water lilies of Claude Monet (1840-1926) or in a still scene like *Bathers of Asnières* in the National Gallery by Georges Seurat (1859-1891) – the kinetic beauty of Greek and Renaissance sculpture was traded for an atmosphere of comparative somnolence. There was also a wish to break the body down, and to explore the component parts of the human form. Paul Cézanne (1839-1906) compiled his card players brushstroke by brushstroke: his choppy compositions provide us with our first glimpses of Cubism. Subsequently Cubism itself – arrived at just after the turn of the twentieth century – asked the viewer to consider figures along various planes of time: if one looks at a figure by Pablo Picasso (1881-1973) from his Cubist period (Fig. 16), one is not looking at a still of that figure but at that person in various moods, according to many

Fig. 16. Picasso, *Weeping Woman*, 1939, Tate. An example of a further move away from the Greek ideal.[35]

associations, and with all the accrued damage of life taken into account. His subjects are never heroic: they are too much bound up in spatial and temporal forces for that. Whereas the ancient Greek athletes, and the figures of Michelangelo, had ridden – or sought to ride – the crest of these forces. Cubism is always a confession of the artist: nothing can be looked at or understood in one go. The individual moment is shown to have limitations that can only be trumped by art.

Cubism, intellectually thrilling though it certainly was, was not aesthetically pleasing. In fact, with the prevalence of sharp angles, and the sense of a world continually chopped and diced by our own limited capacities of seeing, Cubist pictures can seem deliberately ugly. Vexed still lives, women which look like assemblages of body parts rather than coherent entities: we have travelled a long way from the *Diskobolos*. The Renaissance sweetness had been surrendered in favour of a more intellectual way of looking, and this left a gap in the human experience of beauty.* A great gain in its way, it heralded a precipitous decline: once artists began to break up the world, the Greek ideal began to seem quaint. By the middle of the twentieth century, the world had experienced the shock of two world wars: these seismic tragedies found vivid expression in the screaming figures of Francis Bacon (1909-1992). In Bacon's work, the human body, far from having any tendency towards the heroic, is instead bloody and

---

* On the other hand, the Cubist outlook could be considered analogous to the experiences of sports fans. How do we come to have an image of Federer in our minds? By a series of glimpses: we might remember fragments of points, a threaded groundstroke here, a lunge-volley there – now collapsing to the floor in joyous victory, now trudging to the net in philosophical defeat.

vulnerable to wound – it is more likely to end up a statistic in someone else's war, than to have its day in the sun as part of a memorable sporting event. Bacon's art is all about the pain of dislocation, and the mess of the mortal interior: his spillages and extrusions of colour cannot be beautiful in the same way a Greek sculpture is beautiful. It might be truer to say that they are pitiful.

Meanwhile, the decline of religion sent the religious impulse inward toward abstraction. The canvases of Piet Mondrian (1872-1944) with their grids of yellows and reds suggested that solace might be found in gazing on the basic properties of line and primary colour. A human body had become too complex a thing to look at happily: perhaps it was too rich in unfortunate associations. During the Cold War, Jackson Pollock (1912-1956) thrilled with his drip paintings, whose zany energy recalled the bustling subatomic. There is undoubted movement in these, but it is different to movement as felt by the human figure. They produce awe at the atom's busy interior, and courageously aspire to convey that world of complementarity and minute strangeness that supports the smooth macro-atomic world of running, walking – and of course, forehands, service returns and half-volleys. They explore a section of nature which had hitherto been unvisited. Meanwhile, Agnes Martin (1912-2004) made marvellously subtle abstractions which invited reverence – the worship which Greeks experienced in the human body has been redirected into images that border on representations of nothingness. In our own time, Brit art has taken pleasure in swift and easily consumable satire of the Tracey Emin and Damien Hirst variety. In these works, the dominant mode can be an ironic disgust at the facts of human life. Hirst's pieces typically invite the viewer to mull on the fact of sickness and death. Emin's *My Bed*, as we have seen, is dirty, a thing of misery and squalor.

Much of modern art refuses the consolations of uplift and serenity in favour of a kind of gutsy unflinchingness. It also tends to avoid movement* – and there can often seem, looking at these works, that there is very little to celebrate about being alive.

In our time then, beauty has declined on the one hand, and at the same time so have renditions of kinetic movement. Where did they go? Beauty arguably went in sanitised form into a global obsession with supermodels and film stars. Our interest in movement appears to have migrated into sport.

It could also be argued that in time both would unite within the person of Roger Federer.

Fig. 17. Tracey Emin, *My Bed,* 1998, Tate Britain. A thing of squalor.[36]

* Except, of course, in the case of modern film art, in which movement is extremely important.

THE MEANING OF 2003-7

As people congregated excitedly at Centre Court for the Wimbledon final in 2003, or as they switched on their TV screens at home, it is a reasonable bet that very few had the history of art in mind.

Nor, one suspects, did Roger Federer – he had other worries than whether he was about to make a contribution to the history of aesthetics. By 2003, amazing as it might seem now, Federer was beginning to look like one of life's perennial underachievers. His 'breakthrough' match in 2001 when he had defeated the mighty Pete Sampras in five changing-of-the-guard sets, had not been translated into Grand Slam glory. True, he entered the 2003 Wimbledon Championships as one of the favourites. But he was known only to tennis fans and not to the general public. Even so, he was beginning to turn heads. Some who watched his progress in the early rounds of that tournament had experiences they weren't expecting to have. One such was the writer William Skidelsky, who watched Federer for the first time in his second-round dismantling of Stefan Koubek. He would later recall in his excellent book *Federer and Me: A Story of Obsession*:

> There was a savagery to his destruction of Koubek, but it was savagery of a particular kind, combining raw power with a delicacy of movement and touch. While his opponent lurched and lumbered, Federer danced around the court in quick light steps, never seeming to be out of position. His game was virtually soundless, as if the effort cost him nothing. And this impression of calm was reinforced by his demeanour, which was curiously expressionless, almost blank. I remember that all this came as a surprise – even a shock – to me.[37]

This sort of spectacle would result over time in a powerful obsession for Skidelsky, and many major championships for Federer. After a semi-final victory over Andy Roddick, Federer easily despatched Mark Philippoussis in three effortless sets in the final, and many who saw that match had similar experiences to Skidelsky. So at the time that Federer became a major champion, it could be said that he was also coming to attention as an artist whose work of art was himself as seen on a tennis court: the 2003 win was both a personal victory and the ratification of a style.

Skidelsky's book is a self-portrait of a man waking up to the revelation of beauty. One doubts whether in a different age it would have been quite such an amazement for him. But then perhaps beauty, if it is real, is always some kind of 'surprise — even a shock'. As the years went by, this beauty became a regular sight for sports fans. Federer repeated his Wimbledon triumph in 2004 and 2005, winning each time against Andy Roddick. Superlatives were amassed from his fellow players: Tracy Austin declared that some of his shots ought to be declared illegal. John McEnroe — then, as now, the game's premier sage — announced that he was the best player ever to play the game.

By 2006, Federer had won the attention of the great American novelist — and gifted regionally ranked junior tennis player — David Foster Wallace. Wallace began his piece for *The New York Times*, 'Roger Federer as Religious Experience' like this:

> Almost anyone who loves tennis and follows the men's tour on television has, over the last few years, had what might be termed Federer Moments. These are times, as you watch the

young Swiss play, when the jaw drops and eyes protrude and sounds are made that bring spouses in from other rooms to see if you're O.K.[38]

Foster Wallace was reporting on the 2006 Wimbledon final between Federer and Nadal, in which Federer dispatched the Spaniard in four sets which gave little indication of the vexation to come from that quarter for Federer fans in the ensuing years. Foster Wallace's article – arguably one of the greatest pieces of sports journalism ever written – amounts to a passionate defence of beauty as represented by Federer against brawn as embodied by Nadal. It is a celebration of the arrival of a new level of beauty in the men's game. He writes: 'Beauty is not the goal of competitive sports, but high-level sports are a prime venue for the expression of human beauty'.

The striking thing about Foster Wallace's writing is that statements of this kind never sound like hyperbole. It might be that, over time, the idea that Federer's play is beautiful has become a platitude that doesn't get us very far. It could even be that Foster Wallace, by looking so keenly at Federer, and by writing so brilliantly, has enabled people to look with his eyes, but at the expense of not looking with their own.* It might also be – as we shall see in Chapter Four – that the sense of Federer's importance which an appreciation of his play can bring on can also engender unstable obsessions in some. But it cannot be said that it is an exaggeration: the Greeks taught us that the human body in motion can never be unimportant. And if that sense has been restored *accidentally* by Federer, then

---

* Perhaps it is the fate of great writers to cause laziness in their readers. For instance, the description of Federer's forehand as a 'great liquid whip' is now so quoted that the repetition of the phrase can seem rote – almost a cliché.

that is still an important moment in the history of aesthetics. Our pleasure in the human body cannot be kept down: if it is denigrated or sidestepped by art, it will resurface in another context altogether. It may even do so, as Skidelsky shows, in a Wimbledon second-round match between unknown players: beauty is hearteningly prolific.

But there is another implication to the *New York Times* article: since Federer is playing the game beautifully, and Nadal is playing it brutally, Foster Wallace argues that Federer is in some sense the morally superior player. He writes: 'For reasons that are not well understood, war's codes are safer for most of us than love's. You too may find them so, in which

Fig. 18. Federer at Wimbledon in 2006, the year David Foster Wallace saw him play. [39]

case Spain's mesomorphic and totally martial Rafael Nadal is the man's man for you — he of the unsleeved biceps and Kabuki self-exhortations.' His disapproval of Nadal is palpable throughout. This is often a subtext in the slightly tedious and manufactured Nadal-Federer debate. Nadal is the man of war, the plucky and muscled trier-for-every-point – spaniel-like in the way he chases down each ball. For Federer fans, their man is not just winning a tennis match on his own and on their behalf, he is also recalling to them the notion of ideal beauty, and in doing so is not just a better player, but in some sense, the better *man*. This idea that the beautiful is good, and the good beautiful comes to us from Plato by way of Aquinas.

But it's worth a stand-alone chapter not just because it's a big idea in itself but because, in the present instance at least, it may very well be wrong.

CHAPTER THREE – FEDERER AND MORALITY

If you poll the top 500 tennis guys in the world [about who is the best player], about 499 are going to say Roger. The only one who won't is Roger himself because he's too nice about it.
– James Blake

How near to good is what is fair!
– Ben Jonson, *Love Freed from Ignorance and Folly*

It is the 2008 Wimbledon final and Rafael Nadal, at 8-7 in the fifth set, is serving against Roger Federer for the championship. The umpire calls for new balls. Nadal stands at the baseline and raises the ball, to remind his opponent – as is normal – that he is serving with them. Federer, caught up in trying to extricate himself from the crisis of the moment, initially doesn't notice this routine sporting gesture. But Nadal raises them again: he makes sure that the two of them lock eyes. There is nothing of gamesmanship about the moment. It is a simple attempt on the part of Nadal to establish respect. In the culminating stress of the match, with much at stake, Nadal wants to acknowledge the rarity of the occasion: only we two, Nadal seems to be saying, know what it is like to play tennis to this standard.

It is a hinge point in both of their careers. 2008 had been a difficult year for Federer. At its start, he had contracted glandular fever which had contributed to his failure to win the Australian Open: this opened the door to the now-familiar sight of a Novak Djokovic win in Melbourne. At the top of men's tennis, any slight injury can have devastating effects on one's career: years later Robin Soderling would retire having failed to recover from the same illness. It is a measure of Federer's supremacy at this point that his dip in 2008 under such an affliction was so slight. Still his results worsened. After the Melbourne semi-final defeat to Djokovic, Federer went on to suffer several more semi-alarming losses – in the second round in Dubai to a young Andy Murray, in the semi-finals of Indian Wells to Mardy Fish, and in the quarter-finals of Miami against Andy Roddick. This was an unpromising precursor to the clay court part of the season when Federer is condemned each year to toil for several months on his least favourite surface. There Federer didn't do too badly, reaching the final of that year's French Open – but then as Roger Federer he was expected to do at least that. In the championship match he inevitably met Nadal and experienced something very unusual for him: a thrashing. The score that day – 6-1, 6-3, 6-0 – included a rare 'bagelling' in the last set with Federer failing to win a single game. There were mitigating factors. Nadal has an inherent advantage on clay: as a left-hander, he is able to whip forehands high to the Federer backhand, making that shot – already his weakest – unusually difficult to control. And many felt that Federer was saving his energy for the tournament that mattered most. The manner of the defeat made all thoughts turn to Wimbledon, where throughout 2006 and 2007 Nadal, like a marauding army growing in strength through successive raids, had been steadily encroaching on Federer's peace.

We have become a little more used to the sight of Federer losing in the years since but at the time it was a shocking lesson in the obstinacy of time. Even so it needs to be said – and needed to be said a lot at the time – that when Federer is playing 'badly' he is still playing to a standard that pretty much everyone else on tour would love to play at.

Injury in sport raises certain moral questions: does one reveal that one is suffering from injury during the match? In the post-match press conference? Or does one let the world know later? Federer – as do Murray and Nadal – almost always chooses the latter, waiting for months to pass before confessing to an injury. In this, Federer differs from his current biggest rival Novak Djokovic, who particularly in the early part of his career, has not always cut a particularly gallant figure on-court and is even suspected by some of gamesmanship whereby he will look more injured than he actually is in order to put off his opponent. Here is Andy Roddick in an interview at the US Open in 2008, when asked about Djokovic's ankle injury timeouts in the early rounds of the tournament:

> RODDICK: Isn't it both of them? And a back and a hip?
>
> REPORTER: And when he said there are too many to count...
>
> RODDICK: And a cramp.
>
> REPORTER: Do you get a sense right now that he is...
>
> RODDICK: Bird flu.
>
> REPORTER: A lot of things. Beijing hangover. He's got a pretty long list of illness.
>
> RODDICK: Anthrax. SARS. Common cough and cold.[40]

Admitting to an injury can spoil an opponent's enjoyment of a victory; if the admission looks petulant it can lose a player admiration. But the very admission of ill-health can also create an air of vulnerability which can affect one's aura on the court during future matches. Aura was an especially valuable commodity for Federer in 2008: at that time, to a greater extent than today, he was winning most of his matches out of sheer reputation before he had stepped on court.

In March 2008, Federer released the following statement:

> During the time in Melbourne I felt slow and kept looking for possible reasons for that – without finding an answer. Some time later, during my holidays in Switzerland, I became severely ill again. I went to the hospital straightway to get further tests done. And it was this time that they found out what was bothering me all along: mononucleosis. I had had it for six weeks already, meaning it would normally be over. The bad news is that I have quite some catching up to do in terms of fitness as I am not in the physical state that I would normally be in at this time of year.[41]

The statement, while having the virtue of being true, was also calibrated to provide a reason for the defeat after a sporting amount of time – it was released two months after the Djokovic match – and also to imply that his dominance could be expected to resume once he had done his 'catching up'. Even so, by the time of the Wimbledon final, everybody knew that Federer had been unwell, and this accentuated the match-billing: the Ailing King versus the Young Pretender. Federer had won their 2006 final in four sets, but their 2007 final had been a dicey affair with Federer winning, after much toing and froing, in five. That 2007 win would stand as Federer's greatest victory over Nadal until the almost eerie salvation of the 2017 Australian Open final. But in early June 2008, the question was: What would happen this time around now that momentum was still more with Nadal?

THE GREATEST MATCH

Part of the ongoing amazement about the 2008 Wimbledon final is that it lived up to expectations. Most memorable sporting moments come to us as sudden revelations: the viewer's pleasure derives precisely from watching an apparently mundane occasion take flame. Surprise is woven into the nature of sport, and yet very often there will be some deficit in drama: one player is simply much better than the other, the match somehow unfolds predictably, and the conditions necessary for excitement are not established.

This was one occasion where drama was preordained: any result would have had dramatic force. But the match as it turned out contrived to magnify pre-existing tensions. Going into the match, Federer resembled a great king defending his capital. There was a kind of gumption about Nadal's very attempt: one wondered a little at his nerve. The opening sets – each won by Nadal 6-4 – accentuated that state of affairs, giving Federer a baffled, even Lear-ish, air while Nadal looked raucous and rampant. One also sensed that Federer was being punished for hubris. In the first round, he had arrived on Centre Court in his most dandyish outfit yet – a cardigan and jacket which deliberately evoked the aristocratic past of the Championships together with shoes with the trophy emblazoned on the heel and the number five on it – the number of Wimbledons he had won by that time. As one watched him retreat to his seat after losing the first set of that final, one wondered whether it had been right to flaunt superiority during a season where he had been struggling.

Bundled up in all this was the tremendous fact of the passage of time: Nadal riding its crest, and Federer no longer quite so favoured by it as he had been. Those first two sets were necessary preconditions for the enormity that followed, but they were in themselves underwhelming. Federer had made a habit of coming out in Grand Slam finals with an air of ferocious joy – as he would do against a hapless Andy Murray later that year in the US Open final. But on that day he appeared distracted, as if he somehow could find no relish for the occasion. This was one of many baffling moments against Nadal where Federer, usually so imperious, looked robbed of motivation. Nadal's burly and muscled approach to tennis can seem distasteful to the more aesthetically-minded Federer: it is as if the Swiss shies from so ostentatious a battle, considering it unseemly.

It was the moment when Federer's career changed tone. Since those first two sets, it has never been absolutely possible to say that Federer is the best player in the world. Within moments that must have been filled with private panic, and before a watching world, he had to become another kind of player. No longer confident of an innate superiority, he was forced to fight. After the second set came the first of the rain delays. For Federer, this at least drew a line under what had gone before. When he emerged from the changing-room, he had discovered a way, and began to play with more verve and confidence. This recuperation, though it would end in defeat, was still a magnificent accomplishment: he had discovered the seed of his now-famous longevity. He had made the decision to play on beyond the point where he was definitely the best: he would do so out of stubbornness, but also out of love of the sport – even a debt owed to it. An enormous amount of emotion must have been addressed and overcome in a very short space of time. Disappointment was turned to resolve. Anger was turned inward then obscurely converted to his own advantage.

Federer famously eked out a third set tie-break: given the hopelessness of the situation it was a heroic moment. At this point, fans could reflect that the afternoon was at least not going to be a whitewash. In fact, it was going to be much better than that: after it, came the famous fourth set where Federer saved two match points, including one where Federer threaded an apparently impossible backhand down the line. This shot alone, the Federer Moment *par excellence*, still stands as one of his great achievements: both physically, in keeping a steady wrist and arm at such a time, and for the mental feat of refusing to be beaten when defeat was a millimetre away.

The match went into a fifth set. A second rain delay – this one less helpful to Federer – came at 2-2.

Federer was broken in the gloaming at 7-7 – that is, in the fifteenth game of the set. And it was then that Nadal, serving at 8-7, raised the balls to share that moment of surprising but unavoidably public intimacy. He seemed to say: *Only we two will ever know what it is like to play to this level.*

Fig. 19. The 2008 Wimbledon final. For some the 'hero' Federer versus the 'villain' Nadal. For others, vice versa.[42]

HEROES AND VILLAINS

The moment when Nadal raises that ball is an indication that moral character is often independent of beauty. It is the brutish Nadal and not the elegant Federer who is sportsmanlike enough to pause in the mêlée and demand that the occasion be recognised. Nadal appears here not as the villain or thug of caricature, but as a man who is eager to recall, and even transcend, the moral codes of his sport at a time of high emotion.

Yet it is an undoubted fact that many Federer fans feel the need to villainise Nadal (and vice versa that there are Nadal fans who wish to do the same to Federer). For instance, a writer like William Skidelsky appears to have genuinely convinced himself that Nadal is in some sense repugnant morally, beginning a pages-long attack in his book with this grand announcement: 'The list of the Spaniard's negative attributes is as extensive as it is obvious.' We shall return to Skidelsky in a moment but first it is worth noting that the Federer-Nadal phenomenon is just one example of a general trend: sport is saturated with the language of morality. A football fan will declare their team to have been 'robbed'. An English cricket fan will naturally think of Australian cricketers as 'the old enemy'.

Why do we foist morality like this onto morally neutral contests?

In Shakespeare's *Hamlet*, the Prince says: 'There is nothing either good or bad, but thinking makes it so'[43]. That gets us half the way there – human beings naturally think in terms of good and evil. But Jonathan Swift went a step further 300 years ago when he remarked that sport is a substitute for fighting. If that is true – and it does seem so – then it might provide a possible reason.

One characteristic of warfare is that people don't like risking their lives in meaningless struggles: it has always been important that armies consider themselves good, operating in opposition to evil – it is the only way to make the danger seem worth it. It might be that our brains, kicking into war mode when we watch sport, do not quite make the distinction that we are now watching sport and not partaking in an actual battle, so that the person you support is 'good' and the other is 'evil'. If so we are guilty of a fudge*. One possible example

* The distinction was illustrated during the writing of this book when in November 2015, the Paris attacks took place. In this instance fighters pledging allegiance to Islamic State detonated suicide bombs outside the Stade de France. Even the most ardent supporter of one of the playing teams, could be left in no doubt that actual evil was outside the stadium and not in it.

of this fudge is the Federer-Nadal rivalry: it could be argued, for instance, that Nadal is more magnanimous in defeat than Federer. It is difficult to point to a single moment of petulance on the part of Nadal in an up-and-down career; there are a number of such moments in Federer's – particularly post-2008, when he started to win slightly less regularly. For instance, after the Wimbledon 2008 loss described above he famously blamed the lateness of the hour: 'I almost couldn't see who I was playing…It's rough on me now, obviously, to lose the biggest tournament in the world over maybe a bit of light.'[44] But, of course, the light was the same for both players.

Nadal, by contrast, almost always has an admirably philosophical response to defeat. For instance, after his unexpected 2009 Roland Garros loss to Robin Soderling he said: 'I have to accept my defeat as I accepted my victories: with calm.'* Federer also is generally a good sport but he has had other moments of irritability which can be at odds with his clean image, and the 'virtuous' beauty of his play. There was his notable racket-smashing episode at the 2008 Miami Masters, and his bursting into tears after losing the 2009 Australian Open to Nadal. These outbursts have sometimes caused surprise in the media, perhaps because Nike and other sponsors have done such a good job of making him seem, as Lucio said of Isabella in *Measure for Measure*, 'a thing enskied and sainted'[45]. Federer often responds with calm to criticism about these rare moments: 'To me it's normal to be upset when you lose', as he said after that lachrymose 2009 final. In doing

---

* In saying this, Nadal was drawing on a history of magnanimity in tennis. There was for instance Boris Becker's famous reminder after losing to Peter Doohan in the second round of Wimbledon in 1987: 'I didn't lose a war. Nobody died. I lost a tennis match.'

so he is distancing himself from his image somewhat: one cannot imagine the man who stares out at us from his Rolex ads crying about anything. Nor can one imagine the man who sells us Moët & Chandon, and coolly recommends Lindor chocolate to us ever indulging in the following outburst at the umpire during his defeat to Juan Martín del Potro at the 2009 US Open final:

> No no no, too late! Stop! Yeah, come on... I was allowed to challenge for like two seconds, the guy takes like ten... Every time! I can't allow that stuff to happen! You have any rules in there or what?! Stop showing me your hand, ok?! Don't tell me to be quiet, ok?! When I wanna talk, I talk, alright?! I don't give a shit what he said, I just say he's waiting way too long...[46]

This is not to go in the other direction and say that Federer, and not Nadal, is the bad guy. Magisterially arrogant though the above tirade is, it is also a self-portrait of a man under considerable strain. Even so, Federer's assessment of himself can sometimes veer away from the image of the modest champion. Of his 2-6, 6-7 (4), 7-6 (5), 6-3, 6-1 win over a young Rafael Nadal in Key Biscayne: 'Making a two-set comeback against a player of his calibre and then winning it isn't normal – even for me'[47]. Of a meeting with Tiger Woods: 'He knew exactly what I was going through and I see what he has to go through. I've never spoken with anybody who was so familiar with the feeling of being invincible.'[48] *Even for me. Being invincible.* It is the language of unconscious superiority. But in a long spotlit career, there are remarkably few of these moments: in fact most of the top players, including Federer, behave so laudably most of the time that they are often accused of blandness.

In any case there is no way, based on what we see on the tennis court – and many die-hard fans appear to forget that that is pretty much all we see – to conclude that Federer is morally superior to Nadal, or the reverse. Perhaps the strange phenomenon of the Nadal-hating Federer fan might also be partly explained by the fact that Federer has benefited from better marketing so that his descent into human fallibility looks more drastic than it does with other players: we shall look at Federer and sponsorship in the next chapter. For now it is worth noting the intensity of the phenomenon. Here is Skidelsky on Nadal again:

> His game is founded not on surprise or variation but on the principle of eternal repetition. Throughout his career, Nadal's strategy has been to find what works and then keep doing it over and over, never deviating from the script. His tennis, like his whole life, is based on denial and self-negation – on resisting the temptation to do what comes naturally.

That broadside – 'like his whole life' – seeks to let observations about style of play to spill into an assessment of Nadal's character*. But here is Nadal's own (admittedly ghost-written) version of that Wimbledon final where quite another person emerges:

* Admittedly, Skidelsky's book is a kind of confession – to use his phrase, 'a story of obsession' – and so one is never quite sure if he is admitting to a curious neurosis or proudly doubling-down on it. Interestingly, at no point does he seem to ask himself whether he has a right to be experiencing these angry emotions or whether the fault might conceivably lie with him.

I collapsed flat on my back on the Wimbledon grass, arms outstretched, fists clenched, roaring with triumph. The silence of the Centre Court gave way to pandemonium, and I succumbed, at long last, to the crowd's euphoria, letting it wash over me, liberating myself from the mental prison I had inhabited from start to finish of the match, all day, the night before, the full two weeks of the greatest tennis tournament on earth. Which I had finally won, at the third attempt: the consummation of my life's work, sacrifice, and dreams.[49]

Nadal is, of course, no villain, but a uniquely motivated innocent. What Skidelsky's obsession really shows is how innate thinking about good and evil is, and how prolifically we are always projecting our own value judgements onto the world around us. Either human beings, or the world itself – or both – appear to be intensely dichotomous: good and evil keeps surfacing. So that while Nadal is busy inhabiting a neutral world of competition, where there is always a shake of hands over the net at the end of the match, there must always be some in the crowd who are busy seeing him as villainous, arrogant, uncouth, barbaric, cruel, or malevolent. This same group of people are likely to find Federer decent, kind, gallant, classy, intelligent, and good.

Except in a few instances* such as Federer's Nike

* During the writing of this book news broke about Maria Sharapova's failed doping test at the 2016 Australian Open and there have been stories throughout this year of match-fixing in the sport. Nadal himself has taken the step of suing the former French minister for Health and Sport Roselyne Bachelot who claimed that Nadal's seven-month absence in 2012 was 'probably due to a positive doping test'. We do not yet know how prevalent it is. All we can say is that in contests where doping or match-fixing isn't taking place, we are watching a largely neutral spectacle. In contests where they are, we are unknowingly watching fraud unfold. But even so our wish to moralise contests is there in each instance independent of whether there is cheating going on.

co-sponsees Lance Armstrong and Oscar Pistorius, most sportspeople are like Nadal: improbably dedicated to a harmless pursuit. It might be said that they are doing us a service in helping to sublimate any residual bellicosity we might have through spectacles of entertainment. It is true that occasionally – as with the depressing example of football hooliganism – the war attitude escalates into actual violence. But in tennis, when real violence enters the fray, as with the appalling on-court stabbing of Monica Seles in Hamburg in 1993, it feels, as it should, an anomalous intrusion.

THE MORAL VALUE OF SPORT

If Swift is right that all sport is a substitute for fighting*, then sport has immense moral value in and of itself: any time we are not fighting useless wars, we are at peace, and our worst instincts are suppressed. In a world so depressingly conflicted, sport reminds us that competitive energies need not be channelled towards murderous ends. Sport, then, is an emblem of species success: as we have seen, it is noteworthy that all evidence of sport, with the possible exceptions of jousting and hunting, disappears somewhat during the Dark Ages when stability was most under threat. The sight of sport – though a boorish one for certain intellectuals – might remind us that we are living in an era of enlightenment and leisure. Tennis is an image of peace, of people cooperating: it is difficult to call this trivial.

This is true in sport at the level of the individual task. For instance, John Arlott once praised Jack Hobbs on

---

* One thinks particularly of the oft-quoted Rodney Dangerfield joke: 'I went to a fight the other night and a hockey game broke out.'

account of his 'infallible sympathy with the bowled ball'[50]. All sports are conducted according to a reciprocal and therefore essentially civilised understanding. Both cricket and tennis – particularly in their Victorian incarnations – were pageants of gentlemanliness, and this ideal can still be seen at Wimbledon fortnight or in test matches at Lord's cricket ground. One could certainly argue that sports have been darkened by snobbery, as we saw in the case of Fred Perry in Chapter One, or by racism, in the case of baseball. But the prevailing impression is one of harmlessness, and even gentleness. Sport frequently provides examples of civilised behaviour, and even moments of kindness. For instance there is the phrase 'good cricket'. This might occur when all components of the game are played admirably, but to neither side's particular advantage: a well-bowled delivery is cannily hit by a batsman and then well-stopped by the opposing team's fielder. There are examples in tennis too: the great Chris Evert used to quietly clap when a forehand winner went by her, and purr

Fig. 20. Jack Hobbs – 'an infallible sympathy with the bowled ball'.[51]

comments of approval. Indeed the very name of the game 'tennis' probably derives from the French 'tenez' or 'receive', and itself describes this kind of cooperation: it used to be shouted by the server to the returner as the serve was hit. A player cannot be anything without his opponent. To treat one's opponent well is to acknowledge this, and to project a certain peaceableness even within the context of battle. It is this which Nadal epitomises at the moment when he raises the new balls in the 2008 Wimbledon final.

One desirable upshot of this is, of course, friendship. We most of us consider sport as something we do with friends, and which tightens bonds. There is a natural paradox between tennis as a mode of civility and tennis as a sublimation of war. In the 1980s the relationships between players sometimes seemed to tilt toward open enmity: the spiky Jimmy Connors and the street-fighting John McEnroe famously loathed one another. But friendship has on balance been more common: McEnroe remains friends with Björn Borg to this day. In those halcyon days before the explosion of twenty-first century sponsorship, one senses that there was less complexity about the relationships between players.

By the 1990s and into the 2000s, rapid increases in prize money enabled the top players to hire whole teams of coaching staff, and effectively run their lives like small but dedicated international businesses. Interaction has shifted to within the team. In today's global world of fabulously lucrative tennis, players resemble presidential candidates with their own machines to run. One senses that Roger Federer and Rafael Nadal are as unlikely to have a real friendship as Barack Obama and Mitt Romney. Even so, the received wisdom is that Nadal and Federer 'get on' because of their 'mutual respect' – that raised new ball at 8-7 again. Federer and Djokovic, according to Boris Becker's 2015 book *Boris Becker's Wimbledon* don't particularly like each other, the suggestion being that the Serb's gradual rise to pre-eminence has rankled Federer. But this anfractuousness dates back to Djokovic's emergence as a jokey teenager who entertained the practice session crowds by doing impressions of the other players: for Federer tennis is something too important to be undermined. Federer has also had a slightly up and down relationship with Murray[52] but really his relationships with his main rivals have a generational gap to contend with. Federer seems to prefer those of his own generation – that is to say, people five years older than Nadal, Murray and Djokovic, the rivals he came to dominate from 2003 to 2007. Federer's relationship, for instance, with Andy Roddick is good. In answer to a recent tweet by Federer applauding the news that Roddick would commentate for the BBC, Roddick wrote: 'Hopefully commentating will be easier than playing against you.'[53] This kind of jocular banter is hard to imagine between Federer and any of the younger players: he adopts instead a kind of paternal tolerance of the younger generation. But Federer's closest friend on the circuit is his countryman Stan Wawrinka, whose rise to Grand Slam winner status over the past few years doesn't seem to have impaired their friendship. When Wawrinka won the 2015 French Open, denying Djokovic a calendar year Grand Slam, Federer was photographed at a football match watching the match on his smartphone: there was no doubt who he was supporting.

Sport in general – and perhaps tennis in particular – can also be an opportunity for flirtation. It is difficult to think of a more flirtatious sport than mixed doubles. A lovely example of this occurs in John Betjeman's poem 'A Subaltern's Love Song':

> Love-thirty, love-forty, oh! weakness of joy,
> The speed of a swallow, the grace of a boy,
> With carefullest carelessness, gaily you won,
> I am weak from your loveliness, Joan Hunter Dunn.[54]

There are also instances of romance in the professional game. Chris Evert was engaged to Jimmy Connors, a relation-ship with 26 Grand Slam Singles titles between them. Andre Agassi and Steffi Graf would outdo this: together they have 30 Grand Slams. Federer himself married former tennis player Mirka Vavrincová, having met her in the Olympic village in Sydney in 2000. Even amid all the missiles of the top tennis player's daily life, Cupid's dart can sometimes sneak in. This is a good thing.

THE DRAWBACKS OF SPORT

And yet sporting friendships all too often inhabit the realm of matiness. With their hollow joshing and larking about, they can send you back to the Orwell-Hitchens camp and its oft-repeated criticism: sport is superficial.

This allegation can be seen in microcosm in a minor controversy which surrounded Tim Henman during his 2003 Wimbledon campaign. During that weather-hit tournament, Henman was asked whether he liked to read books during rain delays. He answered that that would be boring. This piqued the interest of the writer Susan Hill who wrote in *The Guardian*:

the comments of [....] Henman about books being boring set off a chain of reactions in me. Role models are role models and whether they are famous for cooking or playing a ball game, their comments about a lot of other matters are influential. Vast amounts of public money are spent on encouraging the young to read books; how much attention are they going to pay when two bright young men, who are famous, rich and successful, not only say they never read because reading's boring, but actually seem proud of the fact...I wonder whether Henman would have won Wimbledon three times by now if he had enjoyed the Brontës and John Buchan, Dickens and Salinger, Hemingway and Chaucer and Winterson and Smollett?[55]

On the face of it, this is doubtful. Tennis professionals succeed or fail precisely by their ability to carry out a rote task – *against a wall, against a wall* – over and over, during the course of many years, while succumbing to very few, if any, distractions. The probable answer to Hill's question is that if Tim Henman had been a voracious reader, far from being a multiple Wimbledon champion, he wouldn't have been a professional tennis player at all. The questioning mind will probably balk at the edict to practise one's second serve for six hours on end. One also wonders whether with a ball coming down at Henman at 130mph, there would really be time to consult the wisdom of *A Farewell to Arms* or *The Catcher in the Rye* in order to formulate a strategy for his return of serve.

But Hill's complaint is really about fragmentation: in asking why our sportspeople cannot read books, she is wondering why sport must be so separate. A 2009 survey for Tennis TV which asked ATP players their favourite books would have worried her further. Where players could name an author they tended to plump not for the Brontës or Chaucer but for Dan Brown. But both Andy Murray and Federer looked dismissive of the question, with Federer saying: 'I actually read a lot of magazines and newspapers so I actually don't have a favourite book.'[56] On the other hand, it is not always the case that sportsmen aren't readers. The Serbian player Janko Tipsarević lists Nietzsche, Dostoyevsky and Schopenhauer as his favourite writers and plays with an arm tattoo which reads 'Beauty saves the world', a line from *The Idiot*. Venus Williams has a page of her website devoted to her favourite books. Cricketers also have wider horizons than Federer or Murray, and reading lists which might please Susan Hill. The wonderful Sri Lankan cricketer Kumar Sangakkara – with 12,400 Test match runs to his name, one of the very best – relaxed by reading Lucretius and Shakespeare, and perhaps his play did have a kind of temperance and sagacity that could make you think his reading had seeped somehow into his cricket. Former England cricketers Ed Smith, Jonathan Agnew and Michael Atherton have gone on to become excellent writers. It seems that the worlds of intellectual and physical activity need not really be as cut off from one another as they appear to be.

Perhaps then Hill is right and we really might wish for a more intellectual sporting world. Many could do without the depressing nature of the monosyllabic post-match interview, where television is compelled to seek wisdom about the match from the quarter where they are usually least likely to find it: the lips of the players themselves. The great pianist Glenn Gould looked back on his school days as a time of 'athletic goodguyism that admitted of no physical, spiritual or moral ambiguity whatsoever'[57]. One finds evidence of this in the English cricket team: there is a wearisome inevitability to the way in which the latest arrival to the team will acquire the usual nickname – Belly, Stokesy, Swanny, Cooky, and so forth. But any project to combat this is likely to run up against the intractable fact that the world also operates by variety, and that people have a right to be unlike one another. If one were to follow Hill's suggestion, and leave copies of *The Adventures of Roderick Random* or *The Canterbury Tales* lying around the changing rooms of Wimbledon, there is a strong likelihood that they would remain unread. And how much pleasure would it really give us if in a post-match interview Federer were to respond to the usual questions from Sue Barker with a chunk of *Henry V* or to compare his victory glancingly to the ambitions of David Copperfield?

Is it that we have become accustomed to the notion that our Wimbledon champions have made appropriate sacrifices – that for better or worse, a total commitment from our sportsmen, although it might mean enormous financial rewards, necessarily comes at a cost to the intellectual life?

Again one comes back to the Greeks to whom such a distinction would have been ridiculous. One is always trying to steer a course between snobbery and the suspicion that sport really could be presented to us in a less clichéd way.

GLORY AND MYTH

Besides, the rigid commitments of the tennis player do not preclude mental life – when one talks of Federer's play as 'intelligent' as one frequently does, one isn't praising a chimera. Indeed it might be that tennis players inhabit a mental world which the less physically gifted can barely imagine. In the rush and thrill of a Grand Slam final, there is a depth of sympathy between players which the spectators cannot be in on, which might be called, for want of a better word, intellectual. Sport involves physical *and* mental pleasure. Once again we return to that moment of Nadal's insisting that Federer take a moment to pause and look him in the eye at new balls, that wordless acknowledgement of a shared experience. It is a moment to bask in a heroic plane of activity, but it could also be seen as a primarily *intelligent* moment. It is also good – as a civilised gesture, as part of a harmless contest that has successfully suppressed our inbuilt habit of actual warfare. It might also be that the rare and the difficult carries with it a kind of goodness which derives from inherent adventure, the daring of it all. All tennis players at the highest level exhibit the courage of not caving in to the pressures of the day: where we would wilt under pressure, they do not. They arrive in situations that would dwarf us and are not dwarfed. There is something admirable about their ability to face the occasion.

Which returns us to Michelangelo's *David*, the best image we have of the hero. What is *David* thinking? It is the look of a man committed to an undertaking – the slaying of Goliath. He is looking off to one side prior to its execution. It is the same look of misty concentration that we see in tennis players before receiving a serve: the eyes are forcing the world into obedience, summoning their owner's capacities. He is a man equal to a gigantic responsibility. In our age where do we find this? Our politicians are often technocrats; our religious leaders marginalised; our writers are less and less read. This need of heroes – as ancient as humankind itself – is met in our film stars, musicians, and by our sportspeople. At the 2015

US Open after a straight sets win in the fourth round against John Isner, Federer went over to the crowds by the exit to sign memorabilia. A crush ensued, threatening a boy near the front. Federer raised an imperious hand and the crush was allayed. He subsequently took especial time with the boy, signing the usual tennis ball and RF hat. It was an admirable moment of kindness, but even so the media coverage was revealingly gushing. *The Evening Standard* wrote: 'Roger Federer is not only one of the greatest tennis players of all time he is, on this evidence, one of the nicest guys to boot.'[58] Footage revealed a somewhat less dramatic scene than the written reports suggested: the whole episode was an indication of how much we need heroes, and how readily we will elevate the behaviour of a famous person if it will fulfil that need.* Whatever Federer might be in private, in public he is not just the good man – he is the good hero. And much of this stems from the fact that he is also a man of power.

* One thinks of Babe Ruth visiting sick children and dedicating home runs to them.

CHAPTER FOUR – FEDERER AND POWER

Me? I'm loyal and honest, and I'm a good person. I call a spade a spade. Money doesn't make me; I make money. Without money, I'd be the same person.
– Floyd Mayweather

Power tends to corrupt, and absolute power corrupts absolutely.
– Lord Acton

Federer's defeat to Rafael Nadal in the 2008 Wimbledon final ushered in a new era for Federer, where he was no longer indubitably the best player in the world. But his deterioration – if it can even be called that – has hardly been rapid. For most of that time he has simply been the second-best, and in any case would return to world number one in 2009 and again in 2012. Since that 2008 loss at Wimbledon, Federer has won two further Wimbledons, a French Open, a US Open, two Australian Opens, as well as two World Tour Finals, Olympic doubles gold, Olympic singles silver, and a Davis Cup victory for Switzerland. That represents six major championships, more than double the career tally of highly successful players like Lleyton Hewitt and Marat Safin. Some of these were firsts: in 2009, Federer not only won the French Open for the first time, thereby completing the 'Career Grand Slam', but also completed the back-to-back French Open-Wimbledon double, passing Pete Sampras' record of 14 major titles in the process. Even Federer's 'decline' has been an impressive smorgasbord of achievement – a sort of career within a career that more or less any other player would rush to experience.

But all the while his results have been dropping off a little on the court, his power and influence beyond it have been growing.

The Federer we see today – heroic, confident and kind – is impossible to divorce from the trappings of success. As with the 2008 new balls moment between him and Nadal, this fact – the fact of his power, and the possible corruption that can come with power – was vividly illustrated in a Wimbledon final.

THE '15' JACKET

Federer's opponent in the championship match at the 2009 Wimbledon final was, as it had been in 2004 and 2005, Andy Roddick.

Roddick, with his quips and passionate love of the sport, is one of the most likeable players of any era. While being splendidly successful by most standards, it is easy to damn him with faint praise. Like most top ten tennis players of the last 15 years he can count himself unlucky in the era he has played in. In particular, he has had a tough time against Federer: his head-to-head record of 21 losses to just three victories tells of a lopsided rivalry. In spite of this, Roddick was an immensely successful player – a former number one and the winner of the 2002 US Open title. Roddick's game did have its stylistic limits: built around a big serve and a powerful forehand, it belonged to the 1990s, and was in retrospect not quite equipped for the advances later brought about by Federer and Nadal. Against a varied player like Federer, he resembled the hedgehog who knows one thing well; Federer, of course, is the fox who knows many. Roddick would play the 2009 final with a hunger that went back to childhood: as a boy growing up in Texas, he would set his alarm for the middle of the night to catch the Wimbledon final. It was the tournament that really mattered to him. After those defeats in 2004 and 2005, his progress in the 2009 tournament was surprising, a small renaissance. He hadn't been expected to beat Andy Murray in the semi-finals, but his humour had won the crowd over: he had stated that when the partisan crowd cheered for Andy, he would imagine they were cheering for him. Even so, Roddick was not expected to trouble Federer in the final.

With Nadal out from injury, Federer had been elevated to the status of number one seed. He was coming off his uniquely satisfying French Open win, where he had equalled the Sampras record of 14 Grand Slam titles in the process. A win at Wimbledon would break that number. Over the years Federer and Sampras had become friends and Sampras, who had exiled himself from the tennis world since retirement, flew in, fulfilling a jovial promise he had made to witness his record go. It felt like a foregone conclusion – but it would take some concluding. The match would instead stand as a reminder of the uniqueness and freshness of each day, and the number of variables that always surround sport.

Roddick, serving extremely well, won the first set 7-5. There had been a similar start to the 2004 Wimbledon final: in the past Federer had sometimes been content to lose the first set to Roddick, absorbing his power, happy in the knowledge that he had other facets to his game which could be summoned once the American had tired a little. But this pattern didn't repeat itself in 2009: here there would be much more of an onslaught to absorb. Roddick went on to secure four set points in the second set tie-breaker; one began to think about the possible futility of Sampras' transatlantic flight to be there. But tennis can change rapidly: three set points were saved by Federer. On the final set point, Federer chipped back a Roddick serve; Roddick whipped the ball deep into the deuce court and, scampering to his right, Federer was only able to chip the ball back in play: a looped invitation, it seemed, to close out the set. The following shot Roddick must replay in his mind regularly: it's to his credit that he has never shown a trace of self-pity about it. In retrospect the ball hung in the air just long enough to create doubt and for the crucial nature of the moment to impress itself on him. He snatched at the backhand volley and sent the ball wide, beyond even the tramlines of the advantage court.

Federer went on to win the tie-break and after that, even during the long 16-14 final set, the remainder felt like a phantom contest, as if the match had somehow already been won by Federer – or lost by Roddick.

The match point – the first time that Federer would break the Roddick serve in the match – has been replayed often. It was a record-breaking moment, which made Federer what he still is today: the most successful player in Grand Slam tennis history*. But like all match points it was a dual moment. The BBC coverage understandably focuses on

* At the second time of my stating this stat, I feel I should add something and say that one needs to be a little wary of it. Rod Laver for instance would have almost certainly posted a higher number than his 11 titles if he had played between the years 1963 and 1968, when he was banned from playing in Grand Slam tournaments before the onset of the Open Era. Likewise, Björn Borg might have won more than his 11 titles if he had contested the Australian Open in the 1970s and early 1980s.

Federer's elation, his leonine head roaring with relief as he jumps up and down, as if he could easily play on. But there is also YouTube footage taken from the opposite angle which captures Roddick's resigned throw of his racket towards his bag, and his weary, saddened trudge up to the net.

This was not all. During the ceremony Federer was seen to be wearing a jacket with the number 15 on it. In the coming days, debate ensued on the Internet. Where had it come from? Was this gloating? It was initially thought that Federer had known about the jacket beforehand – perhaps he had even ordered its preparation. If so, this made him guilty of not respecting his opponent. But subsequent footage showed a Nike representative rushing on court to inflict the jacket on Federer: basking in the happy confusion of the moment, Federer nods and agrees to wear it. This only shifted the nature of discussion to Federer's relationship with his sponsor. On *Sports Illustrated* Jon Wertheim posted a variety of opinions on the matter. Nikki from St Louis wondered aloud about Nike's motivation: 'Maybe they want to project the genteel image because they already have plenty of players with the tough-guy jock appeal, and only Federer can really pull off the gentleman image that can further expand their market segment.' Grainne from Aberdeen was tolerant: 'Only two years ago, after his five-set victory over Nadal, a clearly frazzled Roger put his trousers on back to front! Can you imagine the moments after winning Wimbledon?'[59]

As upset as some were about the 15 jacket, Roddick himself was not one of them. He spoke about the defeat in 2013 during an interview with Federer, by which time the American had moved into a commentary role on behalf of Fox Sports 1. This is Roddick:

We've never talked about the 2009 Wimbledon final. Going into the locker room and I'm at my locker being very emotional, breaking down, it was a heart-breaking loss. The thing that I remember is your team coming in, and you giving them like silent fist pounds, and kind of giving them hugs but it was in a very reserved manner because it was like you were taking the consideration that this was hard for me.[60]

HOW ROGER FEDERER EARNS HIS LIVING

Whatever view one takes of that moment, the 15 jacket is illustrative of something unavoidable about Roger Federer: he is one of the most heavily sponsored men in the world. Forbes.com states that his ten-year deal with Nike, which pays Federer ten million dollars a year, is the most lucrative in history, and also rare in terms of longevity. Federer is seen as worth the money, and also a safe bet. The company is busy monetising the relationship. A Nike Premier RF jacket will set you back $150. A Nike Premier RF T-shirt would usually cost $40 but at time of writing is on sale for $24.97. Federer has appeared in a series of 'viral' commercials for the company, always as an extraordinary man capable of remarkable tennis feats: in one video he faces down an intruder to his home in a hectic tennis rally; in another he successfully completes the William Tell challenge, serving to hit an apple off someone's head.

Nike's assessment has been seconded by numerous other household name companies. Federer's other endorsements include Swiss brands such as Nationale Suisse, Credit Suisse, Rolex and Lindt. In 2010 his partnership deal with Mercedes-Benz China was extended into a global deal.

Other major sponsors include Gillette, Wilson and, as of 2012, Moët & Chandon. On the face of it, his endorsement portfolio therefore gives a curious impression – that of a champagne-sipping chocolate-tasting clean-shaven man with money in the bank who is punctual, perhaps because he has his own Mercedes. In an article for *Sphere*, Laura Archer tried to unravel all this a bit, showing that there is method in the madness:

> He grew up in Basel, centre of the Swiss watch-making industry, so of course he would wear a Rolex. He wants to be an ambassador for his country, hence partnerships with Credit Suisse and Lindt. Bottles of Moët have adorned the winner's podium at the ATP World Tour Finals and the US Open for many years. And there's an amusing anecdote about how, as a schoolboy, he replied 'a Mercedes' when a Swiss newspaper asked what he would spend his first prize winnings on—the actual answer, as his mother eventually deduced, was 'more CDs'.[61]

As we saw in the 2009 Wimbledon final, it is sometimes difficult to know precisely where Federer the man ends and where Federer the corporate sponsee begins. His team watch him unselfconsciously wearing RF hats. His life outside tennis is presumably riddled with engagements to make the relationship worthwhile for each of his sponsors. Past achievements can matter more to sponsors than present success: the Forbes rich list for 2015 indicates an undimmed earning potential for Federer even at a time in his career when he is less likely to win the biggest tournaments. Throughout even an average Federer year like 2015, he was fifth in the rich list, behind two unappealing boxers (Floyd 'Money' Mayweather and Manny Pacquaio) and two footballers (Lionel Messi and Christiano Ronaldo). In that year Federer was also, ahead of Tiger Woods, the most endorsed athlete in the world with $58m in that year. So while footballers and boxers make superior earnings from inflated salaries or big one-off (and usually overhyped) fights, Federer makes up this deficit in endorsements. His salary earnings in 2015 - $9m – were fairly paltry compared to theirs.

Federer has been lucky in inhabiting a world of swelling prize money. But he is also one of the causes of it: knowing the benefits for lower-ranked players, he has campaigned regularly for improvements in prize money for the early rounds of tournaments – a fact which has made him extremely popular with all his fellow players*. In 2015, Federer's career prize money was a cool $97,855,881 just ahead of Novak Djokovic on $96,142,948, although Djokovic eventually overtook Federer in 2016, at a time when Federer was out with injury. To put this into perspective, Sampras, a figure with comparable career achievements, retired with career earnings of $43.28m – enough to get by on, but illustrative of a significant explosion in prize money in the decade or so since his retirement. The trend is more dramatic the further back you go. John McEnroe achieved career earnings of $12,547,797 after 15 years as a pro. This is significantly less than a player like David Ferrer, a dogged and consistent old-timer who has never won a major championship or especially captured the public imagination: he has career earnings of

---

* Federer has now won the Stefan Edberg Sportsmanship Award, voted for by the players 11 times in the last 12 years. He is an even bigger hit with fans having won the Fans Favourite Awards 13 times in a row since 2003.

$28,355,864, roughly the same as Andre Agassi, a far better player, whose only mistake was to play in an earlier era. The near collapse of the financial system in 2008 has done nothing to halt the rise of inequality: Federer might even be said to be an emblem of an unjust society. Without question he takes his place alongside rock stars and movie actors among the era's cast of the drastically overpaid.

This explosion in earnings can also be seen at the level of the individual tournament. To become Gentlemen's Singles champion at Wimbledon in 1887 was to simply win the trophy, a state of affairs that continued for eighty years. Prize money was only awarded in 1968, the first year professional players were permitted to compete. By 2007, equal prize money was awarded to men and women. In 2009 the winners of each championship were awarded £850,000 each. By 2015 Novak Djokovic won £1,890,000, and Federer as runner-up won £940,000, more than when he won it six years earlier in that 2009 match against Roddick. In one sense, then, our tennis players are athletes, pure and simple. But they have also hit the jackpot: they are our modern versions of those who went West and really did strike gold.

This escalation in prize money makes winning a self-perpetuating cycle. Superior wealth gives Federer and the other top players an inbuilt advantage on tour. He is able to afford the best apartments and hotels worldwide: during Wimbledon he rents a sizeable house in the village, and he stays at the Carlyle Hotel in New York during the US Open. As a father he is able to afford nanny care: he can arrange his life around tennis and not the other way round. This is in stark contrast to the plight of the qualifier who must somehow make ends meet in remote tournaments. For instance in 2008, Britain's

Chris Eaton made it to the second round of Wimbledon. Until that surprise run Eaton had career earnings of £2,700: for his second round showing alone he won £17,000. Eaton told *The Evening Standard*: 'There are some places I haven't been able to go to and now I may be able to plan a schedule based on tennis rather than saving money'. He added that a trip to Uzbekistan had been tough: 'I didn't do well and it can get you down'.

All this Federer avoids. Martin Amis once said that sexual success breeds sexual success: the same is true in tennis.

SPONSORSHIP AND THE SELF

And yet great wealth is also, of course, potentially an assault on all that one was before one accumulated so much.

This phenomenon of sportspeople as tycoons is a very recent one. In the ancient Olympics, tournaments and contests were carried on for the glory of the moment itself: the Greek athlete was in effect offering his performance up as thanks to the gods. By and large, he expected to win no prize money but instead wished to be crowned with the laurel wreath from the wild olive tree which grew near Olympia. After the victory had been announced the olive wreath would be offered up at the table of Zeus' wife Hera. And yet even in Ancient Greece the desire for riches as a result of athletic achievement had begun to surface. In the Aristophanes play *Plutus* a character remarks: 'Why, Zeus is poor, and I will clearly prove it to you. In the Olympic games, which he founded, and to which he convokes the whole of Greece every four years, why does he only crown the victorious athletes with wild olive? If he were rich he would give them gold.'[62] One can imagine that somewhere within this joke is an alternative point of view:

perhaps athletes do deserve riches. Certainly this was also the view of non-Greeks. In his *Histories* Herodotus reports the Persian general Xerxes as asking why so few Arcadians were defending Thermopylae. When he found that they were at the Olympic Games and that they were competing not for money but for glory his general Tigranes remarked: 'Good heavens! Mardonius, what kind of men are these against whom you have brought us to fight? Men who do not compete for possessions, but for virtue!'[63]

Even so there is something attractive about unmonetised athletic activity. In Book V of Virgil's Homeric poem *The Aeneid*, Aeneas and his followers pause on their journey from Troy to Italy, where they will ultimately found Rome, for some games in honour of the death of Aeneas' father. This hiatus in the middle of the great poem is sometimes considered its weakest book, precisely because it appears to function as a suspension of the story, a sealed-off zone of the narrative where the main purpose of the protagonists – to press on and found a new Empire – is paused. But Virgil knew better than that. After the foot race and a display of horsemanship, there is an archery contest. After Eurytion downs a dove in the skies, an older man, Acestes, shoots his own arrow:

> A startling phenomenon was seen now – one of the utmost
> Significance for the future: huge events were to show
> Its meaning, and frightening seers one day would declare
> > what it omened.
> The shaft, as it sped among the streaming clouds, took fire,
> Blazing a trail in the sky, then burnt itself out and vanished
> Into thin air: thus, often, a star dislodges itself,
> From heaven and shoots across it, trailing a
> > long-haired flame.[64]

Aeneas then goes on to reward the old man with first prize. The meaning of this flaming arrow is to foretell Acestes' success in founding Acesta. It shows how games in the tradition of the Homeric epic link up to wider questions of destiny and meaning: we shall look at these questions in more detail in the last chapter. Compared with the Grecian ideal of sport, the modern sportsperson can sometimes seem a hedonistic individualist who nevertheless must make certain concessions to the corporates from which they derive the lion's share of their wealth.

Roger Federer, then, is implicated in the somewhat muddy world of corporations. His co-sponsees at Nike include a serial adulterer (Tiger Woods), a confessed drugs cheat (Lance Armstrong) and a murderer (Oscar Pistorius). But it feels churlish to be too judgemental: it must be a wonderful thing when just by doing what one loves the money rolls in and financial security is suddenly attained. There has yet to be a top-flight sportsperson who has refused all sponsorship. Indeed it is difficult to imagine how that might go: if a rising tennis star were to announce that he is playing only for the pleasure or meaning of it, and wishes to be beholden to no corporations, the gesture might not seem noble so much as criminally foolish. Any biography of even an apparently seamless athlete like Federer is primarily a tale of ludicrously hard work, high pressure, and considerable inconvenience, all of which surely merits some remuneration. As the popstar Robbie Williams observed upon securing a record $80 million contract with EMI: 'I work hard. Surely I must be worth some of it.' Federer has done his proverbial 10,000 hours and more.[65] Is there a cost involved for Federer? Probably there is – we can see it in the moment with the 15 jacket. As Bob Dylan said:

'You gotta serve somebody'[66]. Federer serves Nike and his other sponsors, and there must be some element of submission in that: days when he doesn't want to do something but has to fulfil his contract; disagreements about image; irritating requests.

And yet there is room left over once all the sponsor's duties have been carried out to do things in one's own name – and so perhaps reclaim something of oneself. Bill Gates has set a tone among the world's super-rich: a spirit of charity has been particularly prevalent these last years, with Warren Buffett, Tim Cook, Mark Zuckerberg, and Larry Ellison among those who intend on giving most of their fortunes away to charitable causes. Roger Federer hasn't yet done this but he has pursued a laudable route. Admittedly, it is difficult to find any information about the size of endowment of the Roger Federer Foundation. But from the following description on the Foundation's website it cannot be called a small endeavour – especially given that its namesake is an exceptionally busy sports star, who can reasonably be expected to do much more on this front once he has retired from the sport:

> The Roger Federer Foundation supports educational projects located in the region of southern Africa and Switzerland. The programmes on the African continent focus on the improvement of the quality of early learning and basic education and in Switzerland on the promotion of extra-curricular activities for children affected by poverty.... In celebrating its tenth anniversary the Roger Federer Foundation has set itself an ambitious goal. By 2018 we aim to support one million children in receiving access to education of a convincing quality.[67]

The emphasis on South Africa can be explained by the fact that Federer's mother, Lynette, is South African. There is a link here between his charity work and his sponsorship deals: the Roger Federer Foundation works in conjunction with Credit Suisse, and one imagines some shuttling and arm-twisting at a sponsor meeting. Federer has also shown a rare proactiveness in other charitable works. He was made a UNICEF International Goodwill Ambassador in 2006. He participated in 2007 AIDS day, and is also active for the Humpty Dumpty Foundation which assists with the purchase of medical equipment for children's hospitals.

The world has been good to Roger Federer and he has been good in return. It might always be said of someone in his position that he could do more. But it is also certain that post-career he will become more active. As the Roger Federer Foundation CEO Janine Händel told *The Guardian* in 2012: 'The foundation has a long-term vision and there will be a time when Roger will become much more involved.'[68]

THE POWER OF HIS FAME

On the one hand, then, Federer is simply wealthy, with something akin to a successful businessman's clout. But on top of this he has another property as important: the power of fame. Its essence is influence: asked by a 'normal person' to do something and you might not, but have Roger Federer pose you the question, and you might just be persuadable. In response to the 2010 Haiti earthquake, Federer arranged a collaboration with fellow players for a charity event during that year's Australian Open called 'Hit for Haiti', in which proceeds went to Haiti earthquake victims. It was an example of his ability to

Fig. 21. Federer in his RF hat. Where does Federer the man end and Federer the sponsee begin?[69]

wield his popularity among players and officials for the sake of a good cause. Once again, one recalls the inauspicious nature of the beginnings – hitting that ball against a wall, against a wall. It is a heartening thought that so much good can come of something so apparently unpromising.

But fame brings with it its stranger side. His website www.rogerfederer.com is at any one time full of messages proclaiming an adoration that is hard not to consider extreme. In early 2016, for instance, Federer fans could be seen attempting to assimilate their man's possibly flu-caused loss to Milos Raonic. THEREALMRSRF wrote: 'I'm getting a bit sick of reading about his Brisbane loss... like Milos played so magnificently. I'm not happy... Just want AO to start already and our man to get a decent draw. Hopefully you're resting handsome. Night all :).' This is an example of a Federer defeat engendering an outsized sorrow. It suggests a touching, although slightly alarming, degree of affection: it shows again how invested people can become in their sports heroes, detecting – or projecting – an intimate connection with a public figure. The Internet means we can all be like Bellow's *Herzog*, writing letters to the famous every day. To take another example, KAFU11111 was defiant about that same defeat:

> Hello, Roger !!!!
>
> No matter what, YOU ARE THE GREATEST IN TENNIS HISTORY !!!!!!!
> Come on CHAMP, be ready to DEMOLISH all your opponents in AO !!!
> And the 18th GRAND SLAM is yours !!!! I wish you all the best for 2016 !!!
> Love you so much, Roger !!!!!!!!!!!!
> Take good care and stay healthy !!! Al the happiness CHAMP !!!!
> GOD bless you and your wondeRFul family !!!!!!!![70]

We can meet these most ardent Federer fans briefly in Skidelsky's book, where there is the following description of the group known as the Backpack Babes:

> …a group of eight or so, mainly middle-aged women, all with identical red and white 'RF' backpacks, appeared and began posing for photos – backs to the camera – under the Roger Federer Alle sign. In addition to their backpacks, most were wearing RF-branded hats, jackets and trainers; a couple had donned chunky RF earrings; several had dyed red hair. I got talking to Margo, a Dutch woman in her fifties, who told me

that they'd all met in the forums on Federer's website and that they frequently travelled together to tournaments around the world. Margo, who was less festooned with regalia than the others, seemed mildly embarrassed by the backpacks. 'It's just a bit of harmless fun,' she said.

In another era, what would the extreme Federer fan do? Be a religious fanatic? Lose themselves in fringe political activity? Or without the Federer obsession in their lives, would they be doomed to normality, a less intense life? And yet we can also agree with Margo that it is harmless fun, even if it makes one a trifle uneasy. It might be seen as another example, although an extreme one, of the complexity of modern life creating the need for straightforward escapism. The beauty of his play, the perception that he is a hero and a good man, together with the allure of power, all combine to make Federer a good fit for obsessives. It is often remarked that every match for Federer is a 'home match'. In that sense he embodies the final stage of fame, attained by very few – international household name status. Perhaps without the loopiness that he engenders he wouldn't be quite so powerful. This kind of extreme adoration accumulates, forming the mythic atmosphere that surrounds him. Great fame like Federer's is in the gift of the slightly unstable.

THE LIMITS OF POWER

But where does all this leave the idea of Federer as an artist? He regularly states that none of the fame and money he has acquired has altered his fundamental love of the game. His retirement has been often expected but has so far been delayed*. Federer didn't win a major in 2011, breaking a streak of eight straight years during which he had won at least one major per year. He bounced back to win Wimbledon in 2012, and returned as a result of that victory to world number one. In 2013, he endured an even more barren year: a bad back played its part in ensuring that he won only one tournament. But 2014 and 2015 were strong seasons including a Davis Cup victory and three major finals.

Federer has enough money to last the rest of his life, but continues to play. An addiction to adulation may be at work, but also a certain simplicity of outlook: he is not so different to that boy at the beginning of this book, hitting the ball against that wall. His retirement, near now, will herald a life without regular hits of love from worldwide crowds. But one suspects that more than that, he will miss having his genius tested against much younger opponents. As he sometimes says with pre-emptive ruefulness, 'You're retired a long time'. It is another sense in which Federer is a retro figure, a creature of the 1950s as much as the 2000s – one suspects he would have been as happy in the amateur era as in this one, without all this power and influence.

How will Federer's retirement happen? Many would like it to happen after a last major victory against one of his adversaries – Djokovic or Nadal – and yet when this did happen against Nadal in Melbourne in January 2017, Federer

* A knee injury sustained after the 2016 Australian Open forced Federer to have surgery and miss the US hardcourt season in 2016. He is fortunate not just in how rare his injuries have been but in the fact that when they do come, they tend to come between major tournaments. Still, it is a worrying injury at a late stage in his career, although the Federer fan's fears regarding it have been substantially mitigated by that extraordinary 2017 Australian Open win.

didn't retire, and his fans instead began hoping for another such victory, ideally at Wimbledon. The great novelist John Updike in his piece 'Hub Fans Bid Kid Adieu' gave the world a superb description of baseball legend Ted Williams' last match, and the home run with which he magically curtailed his career:

> Like a feather caught in a vortex, Williams ran around the square of bases at the center of our beseeching screaming. He ran as he always ran out home runs—hurriedly, unsmiling, head down, as if our praise were a storm of rain to get out of. He didn't tip his cap. Though we thumped, wept, and chanted "We want Ted" for minutes after he hid in the dugout, he did not come back. Our noise for some seconds passed beyond excitement into a kind of immense open anguish, a wailing, a cry to be saved. But immortality is non-transferable. The papers said that the other players, and even the umpires on the field, begged him to come out and acknowledge us in some way, but he never had and did not now. Gods do not answer letters.[71]

Federer's last match will likely have a similar emotional charge: the crowd will want to project more adoration onto him, but it will have to be refused. Updike's essay shows us the quiet professionalism of a great sportsman. Julian Barnes has wondered:

> But perhaps, when the Mighty Fed eventually does retire, he will become just an ordinary, down-home multimillionaire, tending his children and his cows behind the 24-hour security fencing. Perhaps we shall even stop being interested in him.

And perhaps – is this possible? – his ego is so uninvolved in his success that he will enjoy this.[72]

Certainly Federer has acquired such influence and legend that he will never return to normal life – the room will always respond to his entering it. The paradox is that his world has been so successfully built around an innate skill that you wonder if he ever left normal life in the first place. Perhaps international stardom and global competition was simply his 'normal'.

He gives the impression of being complete.

CHAPTER FIVE – FEDERER AND TIME

Remember that time slurs over everything, lets all deeds fade, blurs all writings and kills all memories. Exempt are only those which dig into the hearts of men by love.
– Aristotle

O let not Time deceive you,
You cannot conquer Time.
– WH Auden

With his laid-back style and occasional forays into retro fashion, Federer can seem redolent of an earlier time. The calm with which he plays the game calls to mind – paradoxically, given his success on the professional circuit – the amateur era. He has more time on the ball, as if in old footage. His Wimbledon appearances in particular can suggest a summer ease: they summon back memories of previous times when life wasn't lived at such a hectic pace. In another sense, he is a peculiarly modern creature: his play is dependent on all the rapidity and spin that up-to-the-minute graphite racket technology can give you; his life would be impossible without global travel (one sometimes wonders about the carbon footprint of these international stars); and he is a man greatly endorsed by household name corporates. Federer's tennis is capable of provoking numerous associations, and contrary appearances – sedate and thunderous, complex and smooth, contemporaneous and nostalgic. It has sometimes been awarded large adjectives: his play is 'complete', 'comprehensive', 'expansive', even 'immortal'.

And yet much of this is surely an illusion perpetrated by the admiring eye against reason, because his career also has a fixed limit imposed on it. Roger Federer is also committing that cardinal sin of the sportsperson: he is ageing.

We have seen that Federer endured a barren 2013. And though he reached the Wimbledon final in 2014 and 2015 – as well as the US Open final in 2015 – on each occasion he lost to Novak Djokovic in a way that felt inevitable: Federer looked during these matches like someone caged by time. In Djokovic he has come up against an immovable object, but perhaps the real difficulty stems from the fallible body – specifically, the activity of time on that body. Even here however, Federer confounds usual trends. He is ageing exceptionally slowly by tennis standards: so far there has been no sharp falling-off of the kind which is afflicting his rival Rafael Nadal, and which has afflicted many of his great predecessors. Federer is still reasonably likely to win, or at least reach the latter stages of every tournament he enters. And at time of writing, in 2017, he is, astoundingly, the 2017 Australian Open champion, a sentence which would have seemed improbable only a month ago, after taking six months off in 2016 to repair a body most assumed would never be able to transport him to Grand Slam success again.

INJURIES AND SLOWING-DOWN

Sport provides a balm to adult lives: it takes us away from daily stress, and escorts us also from thoughts of mortality. But it also shows us the minutiae of the ageing process. Our own decline isn't measurable in tennis results. No doubt we all aged in 2015, but perhaps no one alive did so quite so obviously as Rafael Nadal, who famously had a bad year. But Federer's age was on people's minds at that time too, and he has sometimes seemed in this latter part of his career, to use John McEnroe's phrase, 'a step slow'.

As the Federer-Nadal final in 2008 showed, sportspeople succeed or fail by exceedingly fine margins. A minor injury can end a lucrative career overnight. A bad night's sleep can be the difference between victory and defeat. Every athlete is engaged in a daily fight to stay healthy. Even an apparently injury-free player like Federer has still experienced a dizzying array of knocks and scrapes throughout his career, from the shin splints that derailed him at the end of his 2001 'breakout year' to ongoing back problems in 2013, and 2016's knee injury, not to mention 2008's mortality-inducing bout of glandular fever. In fact, he hasn't really been injury-free at all. But he is a picture of health when set against Nadal who has spent about as much of his career recovering from injuries as he has being on the court causing them. Among modern sportsmen Federer is perhaps most comparable to England cricketer James Anderson in the way his elastic body suffers from fewer gripes than most, and also recuperates very quickly from setbacks. Even so, Federer's injuries are a reminder of what one can easily forget while watching him on TV – the intense stress tennis places on his body, and the extraordinary physicality of his life. Given this, his longevity is remarkable: it is another one of his achievements to have been so good for so long.

Federer provides an illusory glimpse of what it might be like not to age, and there is an obvious vicarious pleasure here: wouldn't it be wonderful to buck time as he almost appears to do?

Still the fact remains: decline can sneak up at any time. Triumph, addictive in itself, can come to seem the norm, until the arc of time stops working in your favour, and begins to bend away from glory. In Ovid's *Metamorphoses* after hearing of the triumphs of Hercules 'which grew familiar to the whole world' there is just such an example of dramatic reversal:

> His conquest of Oechalia,
> That looked like just another, was his last.

Hercules might seem heroic but things begin to overtake him.

> Returning from this victory, intending
> To offer up thanks to Jupiter
> At Cenaeum, on flaming alters,
> Hercules himself was overtaken
> By a whisper,
> By rumour —[73]

This rumour by which even the great man is overtaken is marvellously sinister – it is the sound of the tide turning against you. This same inevitable process is vivid among sportspeople. When a player is riding the crest of their development – as Federer did from 2003-7, or as Djokovic did in 2015-16 – one has a sense that things are working as they should. In the US Open final against Djokovic in 2007, Federer repeatedly served three aces in a row from 0-40 down: he was in allegiance with the crisis-moment and able to outmanoeuvre the worrying circumstance with concentration and skill. Nowadays, the crucial match, the vital point, will sometimes find him wanting. Time hides within success, and vanishes during episodes of glory. But when a player declines, it weaves itself back into events, all too visible in a limping leg, unstill head or shaky hand.

And yet Federer, more than any other tennis player, has also shown himself untroubled by the onset of age: for him, the pleasure of the sport trumps any slight disappointments age might bring. In this he resembles Jack Nicklaus who won the US Masters Golf in 1986 at the age of 46, and Sachin Tendulkar in cricket, who also played beyond his early precocity stacking up achievements which were based partly on pure ability, but also on a superior hunger for the game: many of his records, as with Federer, are related in part to longevity.

For Federer this tolerant attitude toward time appears to have been part of the plan all along. In one of his more surreal interviews, with current House of Commons Speaker John Bercow, Federer explained in 2014:

> I realized very quickly that it's an entirely different thing winning something for the first time and then having to come back the following year and defend it. Once I reached a certain level...I looked up to the great other athletes out there, like Michael Jordan, Tiger Woods, Valentino Rossi, and Michael Schumacher—people who did it so long, so many times and make you wonder, 'How did they do that?'[74]

Federer's reaction to his Wimbledon win in 2003 was one of relief followed by immediate doubling down. This first major championship was longer in coming than it might have been: the frustration of this increased his appetite for the sport exponentially. What is a little decline, he seems to say, compared with the joy of the occasion and the thrill of the chase?

THE LAST MAN STANDING

His ability to keep playing contributes to an impression of what Thomas Carlyle called 'royal solitude'[75]. Federer's contemporaries in order of retirement – Safin, Nalbandian, Roddick and Hewitt – have all ceded the spotlight. Each drifted down the rankings as a consequence of sapping energy and lessening motivation. When the lower-ranked younger players come up against him one sometimes thinks he is condescending to consider their tennis: he is the seasoned player, who has seen it all before.

Up until the middle of 2016, when injury forced him to miss that year's French Open, Federer played a record 64 consecutive majors. How has he been able to play on for so long to such a high standard? The reasons are both psychological and technical. His slightly late flowering – he probably had the game but not the temperament to win majors as early as 2001 – has created a determination to enjoy the trappings of top-flight competition: deprivation created hunger. Further one has the sense that he is playing for the memory of his revered coach Peter Carter who died in a car accident in South Africa in 2002. It is noteworthy that the tremendous loss of Carter, which Federer still often references today, was followed by his first great successes: Federer converted tragedy into renewed focus, and lasting commitment. Accomplishment is often to do with perspectivising death, and having it teach you the vitality of now. But in addition, Federer has not just the body, but also the game for longevity: the psychological and physical conditions, and the nature of his talent, have been right for the kind of career he has wanted to pursue. It has often been said for example that Federer has more options than other players. This can be immensely frustrating if you happen to be on the other side of the net. Here is Andre Agassi reviewing his defeat to Federer in the 2005 US Open Final:

> He's the best I've ever played against. There's nowhere to go. There's nothing to do except hit fairways, hit greens and make putts. Every shot has that sort of urgency on it. I've played a lot of them [other players], so many years; there's a safety zone, there's a place to get to, there's something to focus on, there's a way. Anything you try to do, he potentially has an answer for and it's just a function of when he starts pulling the triggers necessary to get you to change to that decision.

It's a magnificent extempore sketch of frustration. But of course, if you're the causer of this woe — if you're Federer — then there is the basis here for almost infinite enjoyment, and a long career. In the same post-match interview, Agassi describes this endlessness as if from Federer's side of the net:

> He hits that short chip, moves you forward, moves you back. He uses your pace against you. If you take pace off, so that he can't use your pace, he can step around and hurt you with the forehand. Just the amount of options he has to get around any particular stage of the match where maybe something's out of sync is — seems to be endless. His success out there is just a mere reflection of all the things that he can do.[76]

And if one has this sort of gift one is naturally inclined to keep exploring it. Federer's tennis, more than other player's, is rewarding in and of itself. Sometimes when it comes to great achievement it is possible to point to banal or statistical reasons for superiority. There have been claims, for instance, that Shakespeare's greatness might partly be attributable to his having a larger vocabulary than other writers. In a similar vein, research conducted by John Yandell into the Federer forehand found a far greater degree of variety than is the case with other players. The conclusion was reached:

> It may sound strange, but I developed this eerie sense of just how tough it would really be to face him across the net. Just when you think you're getting a handle on what he does, he throws you a whole new range of impossible combinations.[77]

Once again we have a sense of the proliferating possibilities of a unique gift. Federer has so far not reached this moment described by Sampras when he realised it was his time to retire: 'I've always had this little thing I do when I tie my shoes... I finish tying them, slap the ground and say to myself, 'Here we go'. But this time, it didn't feel good. And I stopped, right there and then.'[78]

Federer's retirement will be comparatively reluctant: he will be surrendering not monotony but infinity.

THE ADAPTATIONS HE MAKES

Federer's longevity can create an illusion of Olympian immortality. It is another reason – alongside the violation of beauty – why his losses can be painful for fans. His defeats today are all to do with the vulnerability not just of his body, but of all our bodies. His triumphs are mini-resurrections, or at any rate fierce refusals of morbidity.

We do not accept the passage of time in our own lives – we fight and rail, we try to buck it. Sport shows us this struggle in vivid microcosm. Usain Bolt's 100 metres win in 2015 in the World Championships in Beijing by 0.01 of a second was qualitatively different to his victory in 2008 in the same city, when he had been celebrating by the halfway mark. Perhaps the more marginal victory was in some sense more special. Federer too has shown us how far guile can help handle the ageing process. The early part of his career was all to do with fluidity: he seemed to operate on some other plane which difficulty could seldom visit. His appeal was in imagining yourself into just such ease: what would it be like to casually dispense such beauty, such memories of glory? But since that 2008 Wimbledon loss to Nadal described in Chapter Three, Federer has had to develop new character traits: grit, invention, patience. He has had to learn how to eke out victories, and more often than before, how to handle defeat.

During the 2015 hardcourt season Federer showed that he was continuing to develop with the invention of a new tactic – dubbed by the media the SABR (or Sneak Attack By Roger), a slightly lugubrious acronym. The SABR entails Federer rushing the net on his opponents' second serve: he waits until his serving opponent is looking up towards the ball, and then rushes forwards, backing himself to produce a half-volley. In being so far forward he is then nearer the net if he does make the return, and therefore that much harder to pass. The results were astonishing, and one wondered why no one had thought of it before. Federer frequently had the coordination to return the serve and this knowledge, together with the server's unease, meant that opponents often double-faulted. The tactic contributed to his victory at the 2015 Cincinnati Masters, and to a strong final showing at the US Open. It is not the only change in older Federer. He has also sought to conserve energy by shortening points: he reached two successive Wimbledon finals in 2014 and 2015 partly by attacking the net more often at the behest of his then coach Stefan Edberg. And yet these tactics are themselves concessions to age: they are a sign that Federer no longer trusts himself to win longer rallies as he once did. Even so it is admirable to watch someone who has been pre-eminent battle so inventively with age: it suggests a restless desire for self-expression.

From the beginning, Federer has shown an unusual awareness of time and what it can do to even the greatest sportsmen. Arguably his biggest single breakthrough match was his win against Pete Sampras 7-5 in the fifth set in the 2001 Wimbledon quarter-final. This match was all about time – about two experiences of time intersecting, Sampras succumbing to it, Federer helped by it, a brief meeting of two great players. After that victory Federer recalled:

> After I beat Pete, I felt sort of uncomfortable shaking his hand, almost sad. And later I saw him sitting in the locker room with his head down, and I thought, sure, I'm going to go through moments like this in my career.[79]

And so he has, but knowing this in advance has helped him retain perspective during those harder moments. A sane attitude to time and ageing helps the sportsman. During one's prime it can help one summon one's energies – *this isn't going to be forever, so I'd better do it now*. It can also provide perspective during moments of stress. Who can say how much Federer's level-headedness has helped him during his career? He is well-known to cut an almost absurdly relaxed figure in the locker room, and almost always arrives on court in the right mindset. To accept that age and decline are inevitable is to revel in the good moments, calm in the knowledge that defeat, if it is one day to be inevitable, is universal and therefore nothing personal. Roger Federer has perfected a way of playing without fear.

TIME MACRO AND MICRO

There is a *fin de siècle* feel about professional sport at the moment: it is a twilight of the gods. In tennis, Federer, Nadal and Serena Williams all near retirement. Usain Bolt will retire in 2017. In golf, Tiger Woods is a spent force. Cricket has seen the retirements of a whole generation of achievers including Sachin Tendulkar and Jacques Kallis, Kumar Sangakkara and Ricky Ponting. The 2015 Rugby World Cup saw the retirements of Dan Carter and Richie McGraw. Everywhere one looks one sees proofs of mortality.

Time is a word heard often in tennis. At the end of each change of ends, the umpire intones the word: it hovers over proceedings, lending a curious Reaper-ish quality to matches. Sport, partly there to divert us and distance us from the dark in life, often confounds that wish with imagery of doom: the raised finger of the cricket umpire, or the black flag in Formula One. More generally sportspeople are contained within – and strive in the context of – stricture and rule. Tennis is resolutely binary: two sides of the net, the advantage and the deuce courts, two players, two possible results. The players are subject to this rigidity, and rebel against it with fluidity and movement. So that while sport is one of our ways of blocking out the facts of decay, it also has a tendency to refer back to it. Each match exists within a brief lit hour. And careers – even the most exalted – fade, and pass from view.

Who really minds who won Wimbledon in any given year in, say, the 1950s? In the long view – and even in the medium term – who will mind that Federer, after seeming to be dominant over him, began to lose to Novak Djokovic on several important occasions? The thought in fact need not even be an especially morbid one and might instead engender a pleasant melancholy. It did so for Pindar.

> He who wins, of a sudden, some noble prize
> In the rich years of youth
> Is raised high with hope; his manhood takes wings;
> He has in his heart what is better than wealth.
> But brief is the season of man's delight.
> Soon it falls to the ground; some dire decision uproots it.
> Thing of a day! Such is man; a shadow in a dream.
> Yet when god-given splendour visits him
> A bright radiance plays over him, and how sweet is life!
> Aegina, dear mother, guide this city in the path of liberty
> Through Zeus, and with the favour of Aeacus the Hero,
> And Peleus, and stout Telamon, and Achilles.[80]

One can almost persuade oneself that that 'dire decision' is a bad line call. But melancholy as this is, it also shows us hope: why should we not concentrate on that 'bright radiance' instead of the brevity of that 'season of man's delight'? This is in fact what David Foster Wallace does in 'Roger Federer as Religious Experience'. Foster Wallace looks so closely at Federer's play that his forensic prose slows down time: in doing so, he asks us to concentrate on the vivid detail that time contains at the micro level. We have already touched on the famous 'great liquid whip' of the Federer forehand. But there are many other moments: we are also shown him 'still dancing backwards' as a winner lands, before he arrives at the stunning claim:

> Roger Federer is one of those rare, preternatural athletes who appear to be exempt, at least in part, from certain physical laws. Good analogues here include Michael Jordan, who could not only jump inhumanly high but actually hang there a beat or two longer than gravity allows, and Muhammad Ali, who really could "float" across the canvas and land two or three jabs in the clock-time required for one.

Other examples of this have come along in the time since Foster Wallace wrote his article. There is Usain Bolt's 9.69 in the 2008 Olympic final, where he miraculously found time to ease off at 80 metres in, kicking his legs up and looking sideways in celebration – while still breaking the world record (Fig. 23). There was also the great swimmer Michael Phelps' seventh gold at the Beijing Olympics: in a close contest, Phelps seemed to find an extra beat of parallel time in which to correct his final stroke, lunging forwards in a vast clamber, to win by 0.01 seconds against Milorad Čavić (Fig. 24). Of course these are illusions. In reality Michael Jordan was subject to the same gravity as the rest of us: it was only that he was able to do more within its parameters (Fig. 22). Likewise Phelps did not create a parallel time, he only responded quickly to a tight situation. Great athletes react intelligently: they are masters of time, able to shape and mould it toward better results. Likewise Federer shuffles into position quicker than his opponents, he realigns forces within his control to meet the demands of the critical moment. He is able to wrest the fleeting contingency from his opponent and turn it, not only to his own advantage, but also into beautiful instants which remain in the collective memory.

Fig. 22. Michael Jordan, hanging in the air 'a beat or two longer than gravity allows' according to David Foster Wallace.[81]

All things converge in these moments. They are examples of pure endeavour – individual attempts to solve particular problems. They provide spectators with moments of outstanding kinetic beauty. They are also, in their innocence, and as part of their role within a harmless contest, in some sense moral. Furthermore in aggregate they accrue power to

Fig. 23. Usain Bolt in Beijing in 2008, celebrating even before he has broken the 100 metre world record.[82]

Fig. 24. Michael Phelps (left) in Beijing 2008. It doesn't look possible here, but he found a way to win this race against Čavić, on the right.[83]

a player like Federer who is in possession of this ability – a power which may be used beyond the court towards charitable ends, furthering their inherent good. In their delight, they also provide Federer with a reason to keep playing since causing them is a pleasure in and of itself. But they also buck time by putting it to such good use: they are moments that might really last, and make a long-lasting scratch on our brains.

Finally they also provide a possible route into a discussion about the overall meaning of sport.

CHAPTER SIX – FEDERER AND MEANING

A genuine work of art must mean many things;
the truer its art, the more things it will mean.
– George MacDonald, *The Fantastic Imagination*

We live in a time which has created the art of the absurd.
It is our art.
– Norman Mailer, *Cannibals and Christians*

It is first necessary to address this idea of meaninglessness. Here is Christopher Hitchens once again in full and splendid flow, describing a football match:

> Have you ever seen the pathetic faces of men, and even some women, trying to keep up with the pack by professing devoted loyalty to some other pack on the screen? If you want a decent sports metaphor that applies as well to the herd of fans as it does to the players, try picking one from the most recent scandal [Hitchens was writing in the wake of a concussion in American football]. All those concerned look – and talk – as if they were suffering from a concussion.[84]

Well, so do people when they are reading or watching a movie, one might say. Any sport is easy, even fun, to dismiss: one can even get a certain lofty pleasure – as Hitchens clearly does – from querying the importance of things that other people mind so much about. It is possible to appropriate the cadences of pride: 'Others may choose to waste their time on this – *I* do not'. So for instance Test cricket is sometimes denigrated as the only sport that can go on for five days and end in a draw. Football lovers say that rugby has the wrong-shaped ball. But nor is football immune: the grandly irritable television critic AA Gill once complained that coverage of football was 'of unsurpassed, echoing dullness, ridden with laughable jargon and meaningless phrases'[85]. He could never understand why there was such a reliable television audience for 22 men in shorts running around a park. Everyone knows the withering assessment of golf – attributed variously to Mark Twain, Gladstone and Winston Churchill – as a good walk spoiled. Tennis is also easy to dismiss. In an episode of the Channel Four sitcom *Peep Show*, the character of Jez, played by Robert Webb, departs a game of doubles in anger proclaiming: 'Fuck tennis, it's basically bullshit ping-pong for giants.'[86]

All human tasks if you step back from them can seem absurd. One might try on the attitude of the Martian poets, and observe all the effort and back-and-forth of a tennis rally through the eyes of a visiting alien: it would look as though both players were fixed in an obscure punishment – scared of the ball and desperate to swat it away, but mysteriously drawn to it all the same. Take out the context of win and lose, and tennis can seem as silly as dancing with the music turned off. Any suspicion of absurdity can also be heightened by the television paraphernalia of modern sport. Here is Clive James' take on the 2013 Wimbledon final, won by Andy Murray, in an article entitled with a sub-editor's exaggeration "The Beeb's tennis Brits made Wimbledon a misery':

...after Murray had won there was some vintage stuff from Sue [Barker, the anchorwoman for the BBC's coverage], she having been tasked as usual with conducting the supposedly indispensable post-match interview. "How," she asked Andy, "does it feel to be holding that trophy?"

Murray might have said that it felt better than having to answer the fiftieth dumb question of the fortnight, but he didn't. He even managed to stay calm when Sue asked him whether the fans on Henman Hill had been a help.[87]

The banality of the discussion surrounding tennis – the sense that everyone wants to talk about what they have just seen, but that no one has the vocabulary for it – can indeed grate. With Gill's dismissal of football commentary in mind, one might wonder whether the same might be true of the monosyllabic commentary of John Lloyd or the slick clichés perpetrated by Andrew Castle. Castle's broadcasting reminds us that polish is the enemy of truth: there is more to learn from John McEnroe's passionate earthy pronouncements which place us with startling immediacy into the mindset of competitors. But cliché all too often seems to be winning: when a player like Nick Kyrgios departs from sanitised soundbite he is roundly pilloried for it. Interviewing the players doesn't help: they are under immense stress and must boil down their approach to simple thought processes, and these can be dull to hear. The former England off spinner Monty Panesar would obsessively repeat in post-match interview: 'I just tried to put the ball in the right areas'. He had done and was very good at doing so, but interviewing him on the topic could be a fruitless affair.

At such times it can seem as if tennis has an importance

loaned to it only by the attention we're prepared to give it. We are complicit in this: when we renew our TV licenses or buy our satellite packages, we are sanctioning the circus of professional sport. Sport can sometimes make matters worse for itself by straining after momentousness. For instance, we are often faced with claims of the 'historic' nature of this or that Federer victory, often in relation to tournaments that are only thirty or forty years old in their professional form.

POSSIBLE MEANINGS OF SPORT

But there are also notable exceptions – moments where sport does seem to dovetail, in a minor way, with the currents of history. There are instances where team sports have had a demonstrable political meaning. The fine film *Fire in Babylon* (2010) shows how the success of the West Indian cricket team might be seen as the embodiment of a people rising up against colonial oppression. The existence of a generation of supreme cricketers was a rebuke to the lazy idea that their culture was in any sense inferior to the white people at the centre of the 'empire' to which they were meant to 'belong'. Likewise the film *Invictus* (2009) tells the story of Nelson Mandela's encouragement of the South African national rugby team, and how that circumstance marked a move towards a more tolerant country: in that film, the innocence of sport is shown to trump the tedium and ugliness of unnecessary division, and becomes a powerful symbol of reconciliation. In terms of individual sports, Muhammad Ali frequently tops lists of the most important sportsmen of all time precisely because of his willingness to talk freely about matters beyond sport. His noisy and opinionated career with its embrace of the Nation of Islam, and his refusal to be drafted for the Vietnam War, created a certain expectation that athletes might stray from reflections on their sport into other areas. Today when an interviewer asks a tennis player for their opinion on politics there is a sense in which they are hoping that their interviewee will transform himself from Tomáš Berdych or Radek Štěpánek into Muhammad Ali. But the reality is that opinions take time to form, and the commitment required from the modern player usually obviates their formation.

Tennis tends to become a political factor only when a very prominent player rises of out of a smaller country. In Britain we are used to Andy Murray. An amusing episode of the Armando Iannucci sitcom *The Thick of It* shows the hapless staff at DoSAC (the Department of Social Affairs and Citizenship) fudging the hiring of Murray to front a campaign. Likewise in the real world, Murray's Twitter remarks in favour of Scottish independence received much coverage; Murray later said he regretted his intervention. As a Swiss national, Federer has sometimes been an emblem of national pride: it was much reported after his 2003 Wimbledon victory that he was gifted a Swiss cow by his home town of Basel. Sometimes the country's national politicians try to get in on the act, and bask in his reflective glow. Federer was recently pictured with prominent Swiss politician Alain Berset, a member of the Swiss Federal Council. Likewise, both Justice Minister Simonetta Sommaruga and then-sports minister Ueli Maurer had front row seats when Federer helped Switzerland to its first Davis Cup win in 2014. Inevitably, Federer has been asked whether he would ever run for office:

I don't think so. I'm more into, in general, helping people... We're living on the same world, you know? And not alone. Sometimes people forget. This is why we have fights all over the world. Of course you can't stop them, but still pick an issue, maybe in the future. Of course it goes into politics a little bit. Maybe. . . . But I don't really see this sort of role. I'd like to be more of an ambassador.[88]

Roger Federer is more comfortable with corporations and with NGOs than with governments. He is, as we saw in Chapter Four, part of a more general trend that sees government as likely to be less successful than private money in 'helping people'.

COMPETING NARRATIVES

Some commentators have sought to saddle sport with other meanings too. For some it has connotations of existential struggle. Geoff Dyer saw the famous first-round match at the 2010 Wimbledon Championships between John Isner and Nicolas Mahut, which Isner eventually won 6–4, 3–6, 6–7$^{(7-9)}$, 7–6$^{(7-3)}$, 70–68, as being about keeping non-existence at bay. Dyer wrote of the 'life-like peculiarities of the tennis scoring system whereby sudden death and perpetual extension are inextricably paired'[89]. This is a stretch. In reality, sport gives us access to joy and to despair – but while its joy is real, and all to do with the real delight of the physical world, the despair is cosy compared with what might afflict you beyond the contest itself. After a defeat, the newspapers will invariably find a picture of Federer looking down at the ground regretfully. These pictures are comparable to the look on Adam's face in

Masaccio's famous fresco of the Fall in the Brancacci Chapel in Florence (Fig. 25). But whereas Adam and Eve are mourning the fact of death having come into the world, a Federer defeat is not a big deal, eventually even to Federer. The joy of victory is authentic joy; the despair of defeat is not authentic despair.

Sport cushions us from the genuinely dark, and offers us the undeniably bright: it is deathless drama. In this it is like theatre itself, where the bodies on the stage, though we might briefly grieve at the idea of their death, are not dead at all.

Fig. 25. Adam and Eve, Masaccio, Brancacci Chapel. An image of authentic despair.[90]

This drama is distributed both within the individual matches and across whole careers. Federer's career divides into lots of different mini-narratives, variations upon defeat and victory – with various adjectives applied. We might have thumping, deserved, plucky, unexpected defeats, for instance – and similar adjectives might be applied to players' victories. Federer's career doesn't fit easily into any easy description. Federer has shown brave fight, but he has also had several strange unravellings at critical moments. He is notably successful but has endured disappointing losses; he has been magnanimous in victory and on rare occasions petulant in defeat. His career is long enough to admit many competing narratives: he is a window onto the complicated nature of the world. There is a Rolex ad featuring Federer which shows him staring moodily out of a café window, lost in Hamlet-like thoughts. And perhaps he is – because we all are – as difficult to pin down as Shakespeare's character, full of contradictions and discrepancies that preclude easy explanations.

And it was with Shakespeare in mind that Keats described the idea of negative capability:

> … it struck me what quality went to form a Man of Achieve-ment, especially in Literature, and which Shakespeare possessed so enormously – I mean Negative Capability, that is, when a man is capable of being in uncertainties, mysteries, doubts, without any irritable reaching after fact and reason.[91]

In Literature, yes, but also – to follow Keats in capitalising the significant noun – in Sport. It was Andre Agassi who said that whenever he took to the court, he knew he might lose, but played to win, and in fact all sportspeople – particularly those like Federer who play for a long time – are able to reconcile this uncertainty, and yet continue to play. Roger Federer has been able to shrug off his losses for the sake of some larger purpose.

UPON TRANSIENCE AND EPIPHANIES

The individual victory, then, can seem more transient than the team victory since it is harder to invest with collective meaning. But there is nothing essential about even an apparently unmissable event: you can skip a major final and not feel the loss particularly.

Tennis might therefore be said to belong to what Thomas Carlyle called 'the empire of mode'[92] – it is implicated in the transience of human affairs. But then, what isn't? Either everything matters, or nothing does. The twin facts of the passage of time and the scale of the universe are so astonishing, and so much a part of our condition, that we can hardly bear to look at them. But evanescence is strikingly democratic: things we might think of as 'important' – whether it be the first night of a play by a revered author, a debate in Parliament, or the giving out of an important prize – are all subject to the same laws of transience that corrupt apparently trivial sporting contests. For instance, a picture like *The Coronation of Napoleon* by Jacques-Louis David has much in common with newspaper images we see of tennis players performing before enormous crowds. There is the same sense of occasion, of watching faces homogenised by being part of a large audience, and of protagonists rising to meet an occasion. Since at least the Renaissance, we have had the capacity to step back from pageantry and begin to see through it. In Thomas More's epigram 'On the King and the Peasant', a forest-bred peasant goes to town and witnesses a royal procession. The King goes by and the crowd proclaims: 'Long live the king!' The peasant looks up at the ruler but cannot identify kingliness in him. He asks 'Where is the king? Where is the king?'

> And one of the bystanders replied, 'There he is, the one mounted high on that horse over there.' The peasant said, 'Is that the king? I think you are fooling me. He seems to me to be a man in an embroidered garment.'[93]

Fig. 26. *The Coronation of Napoleon*, Jacques-Louis David (1807), Louvre.[94]

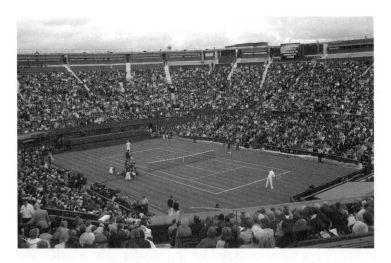

Fig. 27. Federer at Wimbledon. This image is in some ways comparable to *The Coronation of Napoleon*.[95]

So that when someone like Christopher Hitchens questions the value of sport, he is really asking, 'Where is the king?' And the absurdity of our endeavours – sporting or political – comes precisely from transience, the fact that eventually death shall come and sweep all this away. Even art, the human pursuit which most aspires to permanence, does not escape time. It is true that there are some poets – Homer or Hesiod, for instance – who have lasted an extraordinarily long while, and will continue to do so while there is a civilisation like ours intent on preserving them. But many other poets – the bulk of Sappho, most of Sophocles – were not preserved, perhaps were not even thought worth preserving. Poems lose relevance; books go out of print. The sheer rush and contention of any given minute makes a short life expectancy the norm for most art works. Of all the arts, tennis probably has most in common with ballet. In a recent version of

Tchaikovsky's *Sleeping Beauty* by Matthew Bourne at Sadler's Wells it appeared perfectly natural to have a sequence where dancers wielded tennis rackets. But that production too has passed.

Sport then is not necessarily invalidated by its short lifespan. But is there any way round the depressing transience of things? It is worth looking again at Foster Wallace's Federer Moments. Any event in reality, any contest or work of art, is only as good as the impression it makes on the mind. In the last chapter we looked at instances of compressed achievement, where a sportsperson does something particularly extra-ordinary in a moment of sudden inspiration – but which could not have been done without a lifetime's dedication behind it. It was considered then as both a motivation for Federer to continue to play, and as a compensation for the passage of time. The texture of the individual moment will now be considered in terms of meaning.

In 2010, the Wimbledon Championships for the first time appointed a tournament poet laureate: the job went to the performance poet Matt Harvey. His poem 'Thwok', with its cunning rhymes and spirited rhythms, is a fun approximation of tennis as it is experienced by the viewer in the present tense. Here is the first stanza:

> bounce bounce bounce bounce
> thwackety wackety zingety ping
> hittety backety pingety zang
> wack, thwok, thwack, pok,
> thwikety, thwekity, thwokity, thwakity
> cover the court with alarming alacrity
> smackety dink, smackety dink

> boshety bashity crotchety crashety
> up loops a lob with a teasing temerity
> leaps in the air in defiance of gravity
> puts it away with a savage severity
> coupled with suavity
> nice
> 15-love
> (reaches for towel with a certain serenity)[96]

It might be objected that this poem is slightly too busy and therefore misrepresents the real rhythm of a tennis rally: its clacking rapidity bears little resemblance to the lag and swoosh of an actual point. However, it is an attempt to condense the moment into a poetic impression of the viewer's lived experience. In moments like this, when we are truly concentrating on something external to us, partly because we have convinced ourselves we mind supremely about the result, we are paying attention to the world in a way we might not ordinarily manage. When we are invested in the minutiae of a line call, or observing with hunger the way in which our player's footwork is on a given day, we are basking in the phenomena of reality.

Attentiveness is inherently meaningful: it involves paying homage to the world. In *Stephen Hero*, Joyce's first draft of his 1914-15 autobiographical novel *A Portrait of the Artist as a Young Man*, there is a description of the Joycean epiphany:

> By an epiphany he meant a sudden spiritual manifestation, whether in the vulgarity of speech or of gesture or in a memorable phase of the mind itself. He believed that it was for the man of letters to record these epiphanies with extreme

care, seeing that they themselves are the most delicate and evanescent of moments.[97]

In watching Roger Federer wristily skip into position to hit a forehand, or retrieve an unlikely backhand volley, we enter memorable phases of the mind. The viewer experiences a heightened appreciation of motion, change, human possibility, and human will: it is an opportunity for a deeper appreciation of reality. If this seems too exalted, it is worth noting that for Joyce the epiphany might especially arrive during 'the vulgarity of speech'. Joyce is – like all great writers – profoundly opposed to snobbery. In his work, the messiness in life is asserted to be glorious. Foster Wallace is doing the same thing when he begins his article with that description of a Federer Moment – 'where the jaw drops and the eye protrudes'. In watching tennis, Foster Wallace experienced reality impinging with unusual grace and to an unusual extent. Skidelsky also has a description of such a moment of a stop-volley against Djokovic at the World Tour Finals:

> It was obvious that I could never play a shot like that, a shot, remember, that was more or less routine for Federer. If the ball was hit towards me with such force, I would be lucky to get my racket to it, let alone get in the court, let alone to a part of the court, where Djokovic, one of the fastest people in the world round a tennis court, couldn't reach it.

In one sense this isn't quite Joycean in so far as it is couched in somewhat self-regarding language: the reader cannot really be made to mind about the quality of Skidelsky's own stop volley as much as the quality of Federer's. However, he is undoubtedly looking in detail at the world, attaining a measure of the pace and skill required: the physics of things is encountered anew. Skidelsky also makes the case for Federer's play to be classed not as beautiful but as 'sublime'. Up close, Federer exhibits not so much seamlessness as a thunderous effort: his 'great liquid whip' of a forehand is not liquid at all, but an episode of controlled violence. And indeed when Skidelsky writes about Federer he can come near to Wordsworth's definition of poetry as 'emotion recollected in tranquillity'[98]. Our notions of beauty too often veer off toward abstraction. When we confront the shape of reality in one of Joyce's epiphanies it will seem both absolute and anfractuous – undeniable, but not quite what we expected. It has the taste of revelation, and the nature of that is that you never could have guessed its feel beforehand. To look closely at the world is to go beyond beauty into something tougher and stranger, to bump up against the actual structures of life. And the world is so steeped in this quality that this experience is possible anywhere – in woodland, in an urban setting, before the sea, and even beside a tennis court.

INTIMATIONS OF THE CELESTIAL

The hardest thing is to look at the world without fear: to praise the world has never been as easy as we would like. But sport by its simplicity and its innocence can retrieve for us an almost Eden-like freshness. A cricket fan was once asked whether there is cricket in Heaven. 'Of course,' he replied. 'It wouldn't be Heaven otherwise, would it?' Golf forms an important part of PG Wodehouse's Edenic novels. Here is the opening to his short story 'Ordeal by Golf':

A pleasant breeze played among the trees on the terrace outside the Marvis Bay Golf and Country Club. It ruffled the leaves and cooled the forehead of the Oldest Member, who, as was his custom of a Saturday afternoon, sat in the shade on a rocking-chair, observing the younger generation as it hooked and sliced in the valley below. The eye of the Oldest Member was thoughtful and reflective. When it looked into yours it saw in it that perfect peace, that peace beyond understanding, which comes at its maximum only to the man who has given up golf.[99]

The Oldest Member might be in Heaven to have quit golf, but there is no serious doubt that we are in Heaven anyhow: we are there because of the sense of drift and leisure, the pleasant knowledge of sport taking place nearby. A similar example can be found in the poetry of John Betjeman, where a simple description of an ideal golf game, leads the reader towards a magnificent realisation:

A steady putt and then it went
Oh, most surely in.
The very turf rejoiced to see
That quite unprecedented three.

Ah! Seaweed smells from sandy caves
And thyme and mist in whiffs,
In-coming tide, Atlantic waves
Slapping the sunny cliffs,
Lark song and sea sounds in the air
And splendour, splendour everywhere.[100]

Splendour, splendour everywhere. Sport at its best can teach us to approach this sensation. Federer has often stated in interview that he believes in God – as a Catholic, he counts the day he met the Pope as among his best. It is not altogether surprising that he does: he is, as Foster Wallace says, 'of light'. But we do not have to play to his level to experience the agreeable idea that no viable heaven could be solemn and that it would need to have its stretches of play: we can go there in imagination when we watch him. 'If all the year were playing holidays/ to sport would be as tedious as to work'[101], says Prince Harry in Shakespeare's *Henry IV, Part I*. But overwork is also reprehensible. Perhaps to be human was never particularly intended to be a serious endeavour. 'When we are on our best behaviour we are not always at our best,'[102] as Alan Bennett once wrote in relation to Kafka. When we are shouting at our TV screens, or biting our nails during a tie-break, cheering for Federer over Nadal, or vice versa, we are being just as human as when we are making some grave confession, or intoning our political opinions. We are offering up to our world an experience of innocent joy. In his great retelling of the mystery plays, Tony Harrison has the Magi come to the Christ-cradle not with gold, frankincense and myrrh, but with a bob of cherries, a pet bird and a tennis ball. Here is the Third Shepherd's speech:

> Hail, darling dear, full of Godhead!
> I pray thee be near when that I have need.
> Hail, sweet of thy cheer! My heart would bleed
>   To see thee sit here in so poor weed,
>   With no pennies.
>   Hail! Put forth thy hand.

> I bring thee but a ball:
> Have and play thee withall,
> And go to the tennis.[103]

But a ball. The weighting of that feels right.

Our condition is to grow weary of solemnity, and to lose ourselves from time to time in childish fascination with colours and shapes, and expend our energy on some apparently unimportant task.

There are moments when the best we have to offer is an interest in tennis.

TWO CULTURES/ONE CULTURE

But of course we oughtn't take this too far. Because Shakespeare's Prince Harry is also right that we do tire of play. Watch too much of it and after a while you are shutting out the variety of the world.

It was CP Snow who in his 1959 lecture 'Two Cultures' observed that a deep division had arisen among intelligent people: some, he observed, took an interest in the humanities while others were knowledgeable in the sciences. Snow's point was that the paths of the two camps seldom crossed. One might be exceptionally knowledgeable about Tolstoy while knowing nothing whatsoever about the second law of thermodynamics. This polarisation may never have been as marked as Snow pretended. Even if it was, it has closed in recent years. We now have numerous and highly readable science books for the general reader by poetry-savvy writers such as Stephen Jay Gould and Richard Dawkins, and magnificent plays about science by the likes of Tom Stoppard and Michael Frayn.

But while one split has been repaired another wall, equally artificial, has been erected between popular and high culture. This can be seen in the high-handed dismissals of sport by certain intellectuals, and sometimes in the narrow outlook of sports fans. But again this state of affairs might be exaggerated. At the highest level we sometimes see thoughtful types who are highly rounded characters. Whether it be the thoughtful kindness of Jordan Spieth, or the eloquence of former players like John McEnroe or cricketer Mike Atherton, there are hints of a world with fewer boundaries, more along the lines of the Greek model. Recently, in the lead-up to the 2016 Australian Open, Novak Djokovic was quoted as saying: 'I think, for me, a holistic approach to life is everything. So I can't separate myself and my being, physically, from mentally from emotionally from spiritually. It's all one person. Novak Djokovic the tennis player is the same person as the one who is off the tennis court.'[104]

Which brings us back to the beginning – to Pindar. Djokovic's remarks are strikingly similar to those of the classical scholar HDF Kitto who once wrote:

> To Pindar, physical, moral and intellectual excellence – and, be it added, plain Wealth – were all parts of the one whole…[105]

But Kitto explains that this ideal was disintegrating even as Pindar was writing. It has probably never existed as much as it should have. Twenty years after Pindar died, Euripides was pillorying Olympic victors for being men of mere brawn and no mind. If this ideal is to some extent fragmented also in our time, why should we not seek to bring it back, and steer a middle course between complete rejection of sport, and exclusive obsession about it? To do so might be to find correspondences to cherish and an augmented faith in life: beauty and goodness are, to say the least, precious things, and we should look for them wherever we can.

And this returns us also to the beginning of this book.

Federer's 17th Grand Slam victory came against Andy Murray in that match at Wimbledon in 2012. Murray won the first set 6-4 but Federer rebounded to win the next two sets with relative comfort: 7-5, 6-3. He served for the match at 5-3, 40-30. Having missed one championship point with a netted backhand, Federer hit a serve deep to the Murray forehand. Murray hit it back but with no real depth. It was a straightforward task for Federer to whip a forehand deep and to Murray's right. Murray scrambled sideways to hit a forehand crosscourt, but it flew long. Watching back the footage one wants to rush into the frame and inform Murray that he will win the Olympics in a few weeks' time, the US Open later that year, and Wimbledon the following year. But even that, you suspect, might not relieve him of his misery, as he trudges forward, shoulders slumped. But Federer is twisting to see where the ball has landed. Collapsing with joy, he lets his right leg buckle slightly, all his work culminating in a moment of dainty ungainliness. He crinkles to the ground.

It would not be good to be without this – without sport. There are many reasons why this is so. Sport is one of the avenues by which a long procession of human beings have sought to make memorable moments. The sporting arena, though a boisterous place, is not a place which precludes beauty, as David Foster Wallace knew: a sporting contest is a valuable zone of creativity. And where inspiration is rife, there is a longing to invest any spectacle where it thrives with meaning, to reward great effort and skill with the narrative impulse: to find in Virgil's 'shaft, as it sped among the streaming clouds' a certain charge – a fire of consequence. It would not be tolerable for those involved, participants and spectators alike, to find that what they have invested so much in can be shown to be worthless. Accordingly, the human mind cannot look at a bat without seeing a cause, or a ball without sensing a destiny: sport reminds us of our need to lend a charge to the material world, either because the world really is in some obscure sense more than physical, fizzing with drama – or because we would much prefer that it be that way. Our little contests are tremendously vivid; they are valid moments of bright life. Being bright, they cannot help but be filled with pathos. They are fringed with the darkness that confounds all our endeavours, the creep of time, the tick of the clock: *his conquest… that looked like just another was his last*, as Ted Hughes has it. Yet this knowledge, like the blur at the edge of old photos, only serves to make the image itself precious, and make us more alive to the sense of Betjeman's 'splendour, splendour everywhere'.

In our teeming modern world, we can sometimes seem to be losing each day some portion of an original innocence. Sport is our addiction because it is one of the few ways we have left of reclaiming a simpler life. And at the centre of all this is that modern curiosity, the professional sportsperson: part figure of power, part contemporary Adam roaming their reconstructed Eden, and part artist, dispensing their images of beauty. Roger Federer is the supreme modern example of this type of person – a type relatively new in human history.

And yet he is also as old as human history – he is the great athlete, absolutely in command as few of us can ever expect to be, of that unwieldy enterprise, the human body.

The match is over; one of Federer's last great victories has been won. Success must briefly cede to manners. He rises and goes to the net to shake Murray's hand and does his usual touchy-feely pat on Murray's torso: Federer is tactile in both victory and defeat. Then he shakes the umpire's hand.

These formalities completed, he turns and walks alone, arms aloft, into the centre of the court.

ACKNOWLEDGEMENTS

I would like to thank my publisher Todd Swift for electing to bring this book into the world, and for his encouraging comments on the text. I also owe a debt of gratitude to Alexandra Payne for her painstaking editing. I would also like to thank Edwin Smet for his brilliant cover both here and on my last book *The Fragile Democracy*: an Edwin cover is reason enough by itself to buy an Eyewear book, and he's done a great job here.

I would like to thank my wife Jade for her support in the writing of this book – I think I'm right in saying this is a favourite of hers, and I hope she feels that all those Australian Open finals at 9am on Sunday mornings were now worth her while in some degree. Meanwhile, my son Beau is seven months old now. Though not yet interested in tennis, he had a good showing the other day at toy skittles. If we write really for those we love, then I shall always be writing with an invaluable part of myself for him. I also doubt that this book would have been quite as it is without the input down the years of my Nadal fan sister Bex Jackson – our relationship is a benign offshoot of the Nadal-Federer rivalry, in that we can watch the two of them play and still discuss the match afterwards in relatively measured tones.

But this book is dedicated particularly to my mother Sue Jackson. She grew up in a household in Windermere where Wimbledon fortnight was marked apart as a time both of party and reverence. Infectious in all things, she naturally transmitted this belief to me. For me too, life is different when Wimbledon is on – there is that extra drama in the air, that sense of possibility, the wonderful feeling that while the tournament is going on delight becomes the norm. I still think the right way to begin an English summer is to turn those two weeks into an experience – you haven't got summer quite right if you haven't shouted a lot at the television in the last two weeks of June. All this I got from her, and this book is my way of saying I don't consider it a small gift at all.

ENDNOTES

1 This image is governed by an Attribution-ShareAlike 2.0 Generic Creative Commons licence. Attribution: Julian Smith.

2 G. Chaucer, General Prologue to *The Canterbury Tales*, 191.

3 Simon Barnes, 'Through Terror and Scandal the Joy of Sport Endures,' published in *The Spectator*, 21st November.

4 J. Webster, The Duchess of Malfi,. Act V, Scene 4 (1612-3).

5 This work is in the public domain in its country of origin and other countries and areas where the copyright term is the author's life plus 70 years or less.

6 Quoted in James V. Schall, 'On the Meaning of Sport', published on http://faculty.georgetown.edu/.

7 *Pindar's Victory Songs*, translated by Frank J. Nisetich, The John Hopkins University Press (1990).

8 Still from the author's phone.

9 J. Arlott, to John Berry Hobbs on his seventieth birthday.

10 Ibid.

11 Quoted in 'Australian Open: Roger Federer thrilled by Grand Slam win over Rafael Nadal' published on the BBC News website, 29th January 2017.

12 R. Stauffer, *Roger Federer: The Quest for Perfection*. 2010, p. 8.

13 This is viewable on *YouTube*, most famously in the Nike ad narrated by Tiger Woods: https://www.youtube.com/watch?v=rdWtpbuUEy4.

14 S. Bellow, *Herzog*, Penguin Modern Classics, 2001.

15 G. Orwell, 'The Sporting Spirit', published in *Tribune* (1945).

16 C. Hitchens, 'Sport is guaranteed to stir up foul play', published in *The Guardian*, 20th February 2002.

17 P. Auster and JM Coetzee, *Here and Now,: Letters 2008-2011*, Penguin, (2014)

18 John Updike, *The Early Stories: 1953-75*, Penguin, (2005), preface.

19 This file is licensed under the Creative Commons Attribution 2.0 Generic license. Attribution: Squeaky Knees from Cornwall, UK.

20 This file is licensed under the Creative Commons Attribution-Share Alike 2.0 Generic license. Author: The Cosmopolitan of Las Vegas.

21 This file is licensed under the Creative Commons Attribution-Share Alike 2.0 Generic license. Author: Yann Caradec.

22 C. Tomkins, 'Anxiety on the Grass', in *The New Yorker*, June 28th 2010.

23 Shakespeare, Sonnet 65.

24 This file is licensed under the Creative Commons Attribution-Share Alike 1.0 Generic license. Author: Hajor.

25 This file is licensed under the Creative Commons Attribution-Share Alike 3.0 Unported license. Author: User:Tetraktys.

26 This file is licensed under the Creative Commons Attribution 2.5 Generic license. This is a derivative work User:Tetraktys of Doryphoros_MAN_Napoli_Inv6011.jpg: Marie-Lan Nguyen (2011).

27 Kenneth Clark, *The Nude*, Penguin, 1972.

28 This file is licensed under the Creative Commons Attribution-Share Alike 2.0 Generic license. Author: Carole Raddato.

29 This file is licensed under the Creative Commons Attribution 2.0 Generic license. Author: John Togasaki.

30 This is a faithful photographic reproduction of a two-dimensional, public domain work of art.

31 This is a faithful photographic reproduction of a two-dimensional, public domain work of art.

32 This file is licensed under the Creative Commons Attribution 3.0 Unported license. Author: Jörg Bittner Unna.

33 This file is licensed under the Creative Commons Attribution-Share Alike 2.0 Generic license. Author: Nathanael Burton.

34 This is a faithful photographic reproduction of a two-dimensional, public domain work of art.

35 This file is licensed under the Creative Commons Attribution-Share Alike 2.0 Generic license. Author: NichoDesign.

36 This file is licensed under the Creative Commons Attribution-Share Alike 2.0 Generic license. Author: Andy Hay.

37 W. Skidelsky, *Federer and Me: A Story of Obsession*, Yellow Jersey, 2015.

38 David Foster Wallace, 'Roger Federer as Religious Experience,' published in *The New York Times*, August 20th 2006.

39 This work has been released into the public domain by Calvecin.

40 Andy Roddick, post-match interview at US Open, September 2nd 2008.

41 Quoted on www.swissinfo.ch, 'Federer blames illness for bad form', published 8th March 2008.

42 This file is licensed under the Creative Commons Attribution-Share Alike 3.0 Unported license. Author: David Underdown.

43 Shakespeare, *Hamlet*, Act 2, Scene 2.

44 Quoted in C. Clarey, 'Nadal ends Federer's reign at Wimbledon', published in *The New York Times,* July 7th 2008.

45 Shakespeare, *Measure for Measure*, Act 1, Scene 4.

46 Transcript of Federer at 2009 US Open final.

47 Comments made in post-match interview after playing Nadal in Miami in 2005.

48 Quoted in 'First Federer Biography Debuts in United States', published on tennis-x.com, July 28th, 2007.

49 R. Nadal and J. Carlin, *Rafa: My Story,* Sphere, (2012), p. 98.

50 John Arlott, *Jack Hobbs: Profile of the Master*, John Murray Publishers, 1981.

51 This file is licensed under the Creative Commons Attribution-Share Alike 2.0 Generic license. Author: Historyworks.

52 Murray himself is particularly close with Nadal.

53 A. Roddick on Twitter, 2:33 pm - 9 Jun 2015.

54 This poem can be found in J. Betjeman, *Collected Poems*, John Murray, 2006.

55 Susan Hill, 'A blind spot for books,' published in *The Guardian*, 30th August 2003.

56 These interviews can be watched at https://www.youtube.com/watch?v=99EoQiLBfQE.

57 Quoted in Geoffrey Payzant, *Glenn Gould: Music and Mind*, Key Porter Books, 1978.

58 R. Parry, 'Roger Federer saves young boy from potential crush at US Open', published in *The Evening Standard*, 9th September 2015.

59 Both these opinions appeared in J. Wertheim, 'Readers respond to Fed Criticism', *Sports Illustrated*, 15th July 2009.

60 The interview can be watched at https://www.youtube.com/watch?v=_sBZ47tnCDk.

61 L. Archer, 'Courting Roger', published in *Sphere*.

62 Aristophanes, *Plutus*, line 535.

63 Herodotus, *The Histories*, 8.26.

64 Virgil, Aeneid V 522-8, translated by C. Day Lewis.

65 Of course the same is true of all the players in the world top 400: a slightly depressing reflection.

66 From the song of the same name originally released on Dylan's 1979 album *Slow Train*.

67 Taken from www.rogerfederer.com.

68 L. Roopanarine, 'Roger Federer Foundation aiming for maximum impact with minimum spin' published in *The Guardian*, 30th November 2012.

69 This file is licensed under the Creative Commons Attribution 2.0 Generic license. Author: Doha Stadium plus Qatar.

70 These excerpts were taken from www.rogerfederer.com. It is an ongoing conversation which can be viewed at any time.

71 This much-loved article, arguably the greatest piece of sports writing we have, was released as a special edition after Updike's death in 2009. It originally appeared in *The New Yorker* on 22nd October 1960.

72 Julian Barnes, 'The Mighty Fed', published in *The Guardian*, 15th May 2015.

73 Ted Hughes, *Tales from Ovid*, Faber, 1997.

74 Quoted in A. Eley, 'Roger Federer: I will not be a pushy parent', published on the BBC News website, 26th December 2014.

75 T. Carlyle, *The Works of Thomas Carlyle*, Cambridge University Press, 2010, p. 85.

76 Post-match remarks after the 2005 US Open Final.

77 J. Yardell, 'Roger Federer and the Evolution of the Modern Forehand,' www.tennisplayer.net.

78 Quoted in P. Hayward, 'Federer is the future, now' published in *The Daily Telegraph*, 7th July 2003.

79 Quoted in P. Hayward, 'Federer fall could signal end of Fab Four's dominance', published in *The Daily Telegraph*, 28th June 2013.

80 This translation comes from H. Kitto's *The Greeks*, Penguin, 1991.

81 This file is licensed under the Creative Commons Attribution-Share Alike 3.0 Unported license. Attribution: Steve Lipofsky at basketballphoto.com.

82 This file is licensed under the Creative Commons Attribution 2.0 Generic license. Author: Usain_Bolt_winning.jpg: PhotoBobil (derivative work: Sillyfolkboy (talk)).

83 This file is licensed under the Creative Commons Attribution 2.0 Generic license. Author: Marco Paköeningrat.

84 Christopher Hitchens, 'Why the Olympics and Other Sports Cause Conflict', published in *Newsweek*, 5th February 2010.

85 AA Gill, 'It's a funny old game of two thrones,' published in *The Sunday Times*, 22nd June 2014.

86 This comes from Series 9, Episode 4 of *Peep Show*.

87 Clive James, 'The Beeb's tennis Brits made Wimbledon a misery', published in *The Daily Telegraph*, 11th July 2013.

88 Quoted on hollowverse.com

89 G. Dyer, Mahut-Isner: 'In military terms, this was the epic deadlock of the south-western front', published in *The Guardian*, 24th June 2010.

90 This is a faithful photographic reproduction of a two-dimensional, public domain work of art.

91 Keats sketched out this notion in a letter to his brothers George and Thomas Keats on 21st December 1817.

92 T. Carlyle, *The Works of Thomas Carlyle*, Cambridge University Press, 2010, p. 99.

93 Quoted in S. Greenblatt, *Renaissance Self-Fashioning: From More to Shakespeare*, University of Chicago Press, 1980.

94 This is a faithful photographic reproduction of a two-dimensional, public domain work of art.

95 This work has been released into the public domain by its author, Razzle-dazzle at English Wikipedia. This applies worldwide.

96 The poem can be read in its entirety at: http://www. scottishpoetrylibrary.org.uk/poetry/poems/thwok. Reproduced by kind permission of the author. Taken from the collection *Mindless Body Spineless Mind*.

97 James Joyce, *Stephen Hero,* quoted in A. Burgess, *Re Joyce*, W.W. Norton & Company, 1968.

98 Wordsworth, Preface to *Lyrical Ballads*, 1800.

99 From PG Wodehouse, *The Golf Omnibus*, Hutchinson (1973).

100 This poem can be found in J. Betjeman, *Collected Poems*, John Murray, 2006.

101 Shakespeare, *Henry IV Part I*, Act 1, Scene 2, 174-5.

102 A. Bennett, preface to Kafka's Dick, published in *Alan Bennett Plays 2: Kafka's Dick; Insurance Man; Old Country; Englishman Abroad; Question of Attribution*, Faber and Faber, 2009, p. 2.

103 Quoted in *The Broadview Anthology of Medieval Drama*, edited by Christina M. Fitzgerald, John T. Sebastian, 2012.

104 Quoted in R. Jackson, 'Novak Djokovic: 'Tennis is greater than all of us'', published in *The Guardian*, 12th January 2016.

105 H. D. F. Kitto, *The Greeks* (1951).